SOCIETY

RALPH WALDO EMERSON

COSIMO CLASSICS
NEW YORK

Society and Solitude

© 2005 Cosimo, Inc.

Cosimo
P.O. Box 416
Old Chelsea Station
New York, NY 10113-0416

or visit our website at:
www.cosimobooks.com

Society and Solitude originally published by Houghton, Mifflin in 1870.

Library of Congress Cataloging-in-Publication Data
A catalog record for this book is available from the Library of Congress

Cover design by www.wiselephant.com

ISBN: 1-59605-274-0

CONTENTS.

———◆———

SOCIETY AND SOLITUDE.

SOCIETY AND SOLITUDE.

I FELL in with a humorist on my travels, who had in his chamber a cast of the Rondanini Medusa, and who assured me that the name which that fine work of art bore in the catalogues was a misnomer, as he was convinced that the sculptor who carved it intended it for Memory, the mother of the Muses. In the conversation that followed, my new friend made some extraordinary confessions. "Do you not see," he said, "the penalty of learning, and that each of these scholars whom you have met at S——, though he were to be the last man, would, like the executioner in Hood's poem, guillotine the last but one?" He added many lively remarks, but his evident earnestness engaged my attention, and in the weeks that followed we became better acquainted. He had good abilities, a genial temper, and no vices; but he had one defect, — he could not speak in the tone of the people. There was some paralysis on his will, such that when he met men on common terms he spoke weakly and from the point, like a

flighty girl. His consciousness of the fault made it
worse. He envied every drover and lumberman
in the tavern their manly speech. He coveted
Mirabeau's *don terrible de la familiarité*, believing
that he whose sympathy goes lowest is the man
from whom kings have the most to fear. For himself he declared that he could not get enough alone
to write a letter to a friend. He left the city; he
hid himself in pastures. The solitary river was
not solitary enough; the sun and moon put him
out. When he bought a house, the first thing he
did was to plant trees. He could not enough conceal himself. Set a hedge here; set oaks there, —
trees behind trees; above all, set evergreens, for
they will keep a secret all the year round. The
most agreeable compliment you could pay him was
to imply that you had not observed him in a house
or a street where you had met him. Whilst he suffered at being seen where he was, he consoled himself with the delicious thought of the inconceivable
number of places where he was not. All he wished
of his tailor was to provide that sober mean of
color and cut which would never detain the eye
for a moment. He went to Vienna, to Smyrna, to
London. In all the variety of costumes, a carni-
val, a kaleidoscope of clothes, to his horror he
could never discover a man in the street who wore
anything like his own dress. He would have given

his soul for the ring of Gyges. His dismay at his
visibility had blunted the fears of mortality. "Do
you think," he said, "I am in such great terror of
being shot, — I, who am only waiting to shuffle off
my corporeal jacket to slip away into the back
stars, and put diameters of the solar system and
sidereal orbits between me and all souls, — there
to wear out ages in solitude, and forget memory
itself, if it be possible?" He had a remorse running to despair of his social *gaucheries*, and walked
miles and miles to get the twitchings out of his face,
the starts and shrugs out of his arms and shoulders.
God may forgive sins, he said, but awkwardness
has no forgiveness in heaven or earth. He admired
in Newton not so much his theory of the moon as
his letter to Collins, in which he forbade him to
insert his name with the solution of the problem in
the "Philosophical Transactions": "It would perhaps increase my acquaintance, the thing which I
chiefly study to decline."

These conversations led me somewhat later to
the knowledge of similar cases, and to the discovery that they are not of very infrequent occurrence. Few substances are found pure in nature.
Those constitutions which can bear in open day
the rough dealing of the world must be of that
mean and average structure such as iron and salt,
atmospheric air, and water. But there are metals,

like potassium and sodium, which, to be kept pure, must be kept under naphtha. Such are the talents determined on some specialty, which a culminating civilization fosters in the heart of great cities and in royal chambers. Nature protects her own work. To the culture of the world an Archimedes, a Newton is indispensable; so she guards them by a certain aridity. If these had been good fellows, fond of dancing, port, and clubs, we should have had no " Theory of the Sphere " and no " Principia." They had that necessity of isolation which genius feels. Each must stand on his glass tripod if he would keep his electricity. Even Swedenborg, whose theory of the universe is based on affection, and who reprobates to weariness the danger and vice of pure intellect, is constrained to make an extraordinary exception : " There are also angels who do not live consociated, but separate, house and house; these dwell in the midst of heaven, because they are the best of angels."

We have known many fine geniuses with that imperfection that they cannot do anything useful, not so much as write one clean sentence. 'T is worse, and tragic, that no man is fit for society who has fine traits. At a distance he is admired, but bring him hand to hand, he is a cripple. One protects himself by solitude, and one by courtesy, and one by an acid, worldly manner, — each con-

cealing how he can the thinness of his skin and his
incapacity for strict association. But there is no
remedy that can reach the heart of the disease but
either habits of self-reliance that should go in practice to making the man independent of the human
race, or else a religion of love. Now he hardly
seems entitled to marry; for how can he protect
a woman, who cannot protect himself?

We pray to be conventional. But the wary
Heaven takes care you shall not be, if there is anything good in you. Dante was very bad company,
and was never invited to dinner. Michel Angelo
had a sad, sour time of it. The ministers of beauty
are rarely beautiful in coaches and saloons. Columbus discovered no isle or key so lonely as himself.
Yet each of these potentates saw well the reason
of his exclusion. Solitary was he? Why, yes;
but his society was limited only by the amount of
brain Nature appropriated in that age to carry on
the government of the world. "If I stay," said
Dante, when there was question of going to Rome,
" who will go? and if I go, who will stay? "

But the necessity of solitude is deeper than we
have said, and is organic. I have seen many a
philosopher whose world is large enough for only
one person. He affects to be a good companion;
but we are still surprising his secret, that he means
and needs to impose his system on all the rest.

The determination of each is *from* all the others,
like that of each tree up into free space.   'T is no
wonder, when each has his whole head, our societies
should be so small.   Like President Tyler, our
party falls from us every day, and we must ride
in a sulky at last.   Dear heart! take it sadly home
to thee, — there is no co-operation.   We begin with
friendships, and all our youth is a reconnoitering
and recruiting of the holy fraternity they shall combine for the salvation of men.   But so the remoter
stars seem a nebula of united light, yet there is no
group which a telescope will not resolve ; and the
dearest friends are separated by impassable gulfs.
The co-operation is involuntary, and is put upon
us by the Genius of Life, who reserves this as a
part of his prerogative.   'T is fine for us to talk ;
we sit and muse and are serene and complete ; but
the moment we meet with anybody, each becomes
a fraction.

Though the stuff of tragedy and of romances is in
a moral union of two superior persons whose confidence in each other for long years, out of sight and
in sight, and against all appearances, is at last justified by victorious proof of probity to gods and
men, causing joyful emotions, tears and glory, —
though there be for heroes this *moral union*, yet
they too are as far off as ever from an intellectual
union, and the moral union is for comparatively

low and external purposes, like the co-operation of
a ship's company or of a fire-club. But how insu-
lar and pathetically solitary are all the people we
know! Nor dare they tell what they think of each
other when they meet in the street. We have a
fine right, to be sure, to taunt men of the world
with superficial and treacherous courtesies!

Such is the tragic necessity which strict science
finds underneath our domestic and neighborly life,
irresistibly driving each adult soul as with whips
into the desert, and making our warm covenants
sentimental and momentary. We must infer that
the ends of thought were peremptory, if they were
to be secured at such ruinous cost. They are
deeper than can be told, and belong to the immen-
sities and eternities. They reach down to that
depth where society itself originates and disap-
pears; where the question is, Which is first, man or
men? where the individual is lost in his source.

But this banishment to the rocks and echoes no
metaphysics can make right or tolerable. This
result is so against nature, such a half-view, that
it must be corrected by a common sense and experience. " A man is born by the side of his father,
and there he remains." A man must be clothed
with society, or we shall feel a certain bareness
and poverty, as of a displaced and unfurnished
member. He is to be dressed in arts and institu-

tions, as well as in body-garments. Now and then
a man exquisitely made can live alone, and must;
but coop up most men and you undo them. "The
king lived and ate in his hall with men, and under-
stood men," said Selden. When a young barrister
said to the late Mr. Mason, "I keep my chamber
to read law," — "Read law!" replied the veteran,
"'t is in the court-room you must read law." Nor is
the rule otherwise for literature. If you would
learn to write, 't is in the street you must learn it.
Both for the vehicle and for the aims of fine arts
you must frequent the public square. The people,
and not the college, is the writer's home. A scholar
is a candle which the love and desire of all men
will light. Never his lands or his rents, but the
power to charm the disguised soul that sits veiled
under this bearded and that rosy visage is his rent
and ration. His products are as needful as those
of the baker or the weaver. Society cannot do
without cultivated men. As soon as the first wants
are satisfied, the higher wants become imperative.

'T is hard to mesmerize ourselves, to whip our
own top; but through sympathy we are capable of
energy and endurance. Concert fires people to a
certain fury of performance they can rarely reach
alone. Here is the use of society: it is so easy
with the great to be great; so easy to come up to
an existing standard; — as easy as it is to the lover

to swim to his maiden through waves so grim before. The benefits of affection are immense; and the one event which never loses its romance is the encounter with superior persons on terms allowing the happiest intercourse.

It by no means follows that we are not fit for society, because *soirées* are tedious and because the *soirée* finds us tedious. A backwoodsman, who had been sent to the university, told me that when he heard the best-bred young men at the law-school talk together, he reckoned himself a boor; but whenever he caught them apart, and had one to himself alone, then they were the boors and he the better man. And if we recall the rare hours when we encountered the best persons, we then found ourselves, and then first society seemed to exist. That was society, though in the transom of a brig or on the Florida Keys.

A cold sluggish blood thinks it has not facts enough to the purpose, and must decline its turn in the conversation. But they who speak have no more, — have less. 'T is not new facts that avail, but the heat to dissolve everybody's facts. Heat puts you in right relation with magazines of facts. The capital defect of cold, arid natures is the want of animal spirits. They seem a power incredible, as if God should raise the dead. The recluse witnesses what others perform by their aid, with a

kind of fear. It is as much out of his possibility
as the prowess of Cœur-de-Lion, or an Irishman's
day's-work on the railroad. 'T is said the present
and the future are always rivals. Animal spirits
constitute the power of the present, and their feats
are like the structure of a pyramid. Their result
is a lord, a general, or a boon companion. Before
these what a base mendicant is Memory with his
leathern badge! But this genial heat is latent in
all constitutions, and is disengaged only by the
friction of society. As Bacon said of manners,
" To obtain them, it only needs not to despise
them," so we say of animal spirits that they are
the spontaneous product of health and of a social
habit. " For behavior, men learn it, as they take
diseases, one of another."

But the people are to be taken in very small
doses. If solitude is proud, so is society vulgar.
In society, high advantages are set down to the individual as disqualifications. We sink as easily as
we rise, through sympathy. So many men whom I
know are degraded by their sympathies; their native aims being high enough, but their relation all
too tender to the gross people about them. Men
cannot afford to live together on their merits, and
they adjust themselves by their demerits, — by
their love of gossip, or by sheer tolerance and animal good-nature. They untune and dissipate the
brave aspirant.

The remedy is to reinforce each of these moods from the other. Conversation will not corrupt us if we come to the assembly in our own garb and speech and with the energy of health to select what is ours and reject what is not. Society we must have ; but let it be society, and not exchanging news or eating from the same dish. Is it society to sit in one of your chairs? I cannot go to the houses of my nearest relatives, because I do not wish to be alone. Society exists by chemical affinity, and not otherwise.

Put any company of people together with freedom for conversation, and a rapid self-distribution takes place into sets and pairs. The best are accused of exclusiveness. It would be more true to say they separate as oil from water, as children from old people, without love or hatred in the matter, each seeking his like ; and any interference with the affinities would produce constraint and suffocation. All conversation is a magnetic experiment. I know that my friend can talk eloquently; you know that he cannot articulate a sentence : we have seen him in different company. Assort your party, or invite none. Put Stubbs and Coleridge, Quintilian and Aunt Miriam, into pairs, and you make them all wretched. 'T is an extempore Sing-Sing built in a parlor. Leave them to seek their own mates, and they will be as merry as sparrows,

A higher civility will re-establish in our customs a certain reverence which we have lost. What to do with these brisk young men who break through all fences, and make themselves at home in every house? I find out in an instant if my companion does not want me, and ropes cannot hold me when my welcome is gone. One would think that the affinities would pronounce themselves with a surer reciprocity.

Here again, as so often, Nature delights to put us between extreme antagonisms, and our safety is in the skill with which we keep the diagonal line. Solitude is impracticable, and society fatal. We must keep our head in the one and our hands in the other. The conditions are met, if we keep our independence, yet do not lose our sympathy. These wonderful horses need to be driven by fine hands. We require such a solitude as shall hold us to its revelations when we are in the street and in palaces; for most men are cowed in society, and say good things to you in private, but will not stand to them in public. But let us not be the victims of words. Society and solitude are deceptive names. It is not the circumstance of seeing more or fewer people, but the readiness of sympathy, that imports; and a sound mind will derive its principles from insight, with ever a purer ascent to the sufficient and absolute right, and will accept society as the natural element in which they are to be applied.

CIVILIZATION.

CIVILIZATION.

A CERTAIN degree of progress from the rudest
state in which man is found, — a dweller in caves,
or on trees, like an ape, — a cannibal, and eater of
pounded snails, worms, and offal, — a certain degree of progress from this extreme is called Civilization. It is a vague, complex name, of many
degrees. Nobody has attempted a definition. Mr.
Guizot, writing a book on the subject, does not. It
implies the evolution of a highly organized man,
brought to supreme delicacy of sentiment, as in
practical power, religion, liberty, sense of honor,
and taste. In the hesitation to define what it is,
we usually suggest it by negations. A nation that
has no clothing, no iron, no alphabet, no marriage,
no arts of peace, no abstract thought, we call barbarous. And after many arts are invented or imported, as among the Turks and Moorish nations,
it is often a little complaisant to call them civil-
ized.

Each nation grows after its own genius, and has
a civilization of its own. The Chinese and Japan-

ese, though each complete in his way, is different
from the man of Madrid or the man of New York.
The term imports a mysterious progress. In the
brutes is none; and in mankind to-day the savage
tribes are gradually extinguished rather than civil-
ized. The Indians of this country have not learned
the white man's work; and in Africa the negro of
to-day is the negro of Herodotus. In other races
the growth is not arrested, but the like progress
that is made by a boy " when he cuts his eye-
teeth," as we say,— childish illusions passing daily
away and he seeing things really and comprehen-
sively,— is made by tribes. It is the learning the
secret of cumulative power, of advancing on one's
self. It implies a facility of association, power to
compare, the ceasing from fixed ideas. The Indian
is gloomy and distressed when urged to depart from
his habits and traditions. He is overpowered by
the gaze of the white, and his eye sinks. The occasion of one of these starts of growth is always
some novelty that astounds the mind and provokes
it to dare to change. Thus there is a Cadmus, a
Pytheas, a Manco Capac at the beginning of each
improvement, — some superior foreigner importing
new and wonderful arts, and teaching them. Of
course he must not know too much, but must have
the sympathy, language, and gods of those he
would inform. But chiefly the sea-shore has been

the point of departure, to knowledge, as to commerce. The most advanced nations are always those who navigate the most. The power which the sea requires in the sailor makes a man of him very fast, and the change of shores and population clears his head of much nonsense of his wigwam.

Where shall we begin or end the list of those feats of liberty and wit, each of which feats made an epoch of history? Thus the effect of a framed or stone house is immense on the tranquillity, power, and refinement of the builder. A man in a cave or in a camp, a nomad, will die with no more estate than the wolf or the horse leaves. But so simple a labor as a house being achieved, his chief enemies are kept at bay. He is safe from the teeth of wild animals, from frost, sun-stroke, and weather; and fine faculties begin to yield their fine harvest. Invention and art are born, manners and social beauty and delight. 'T is wonderful how soon a piano gets into a log-hut on the frontier. You would think they found it under a pine-stump. With it comes a Latin grammar, — and one of those tow-head boys has written a hymn on Sunday. Now let colleges, now let senates take heed! for here is one who opening these fine tastes on the basis of the pioneer's iron constitution, will gather all their laurels in his strong hands.

When the Indian trail gets widened, graded and

bridged to a good road, there is a benefactor, there
is a missionary, a pacificator, a wealth-bringer, a
maker of markets, a vent for industry. Another
step in civility is the change from war, hunting, and
pasturage, to agriculture. Our Scandinavian fore-
fathers have left us a significant legend to convey
their sense of the importance of this step. "There
was once a giantess who had a daughter, and the
child saw a husbandman ploughing in the field.
Then she ran and picked him up with her finger and
thumb, and put him and his plough and his oxen
into her apron, and carried them to her mother, and
said, ' Mother, what sort of a beetle is this that I
found wriggling in the sand?' But the mother
said, ' Put it away, my child ; we must begone out
of this land, for these people will dwell in it.' "
Another success is the post-office, with its educating
energy augmented by cheapness and guarded by a
certain religious sentiment in mankind ; so that the
power of a wafer or a drop of wax or gluten to
guard a letter, as it flies over sea over land and
comes to its address as if a battalion of artillery
brought it, I look upon as a fine meter of civilization.

The division of labor, the multiplication of the
arts of peace, which is nothing but a large allowance to each man to choose his work according to
his faculty, — to live by his better hand, — fills the

State with useful and happy laborers; and they, creating demand by the very temptation of their productions, are rapidly and surely rewarded by good sale: and what a police and ten commandments their work thus becomes. So true is Dr. Johnson's remark that " men are seldom more innocently employed than when they are making money."

The skilful combinations of civil government, though they usually follow natural leadings, as the lines of race, language, religion, and territory, yet require wisdom and conduct in the rulers, and in their result delight the imagination. " We see insurmountable multitudes obeying, in opposition to their strongest passions, the restraints of a power which they scarcely perceive, and the crimes of a single individual marked and punished at the distance of half the earth." [1]

Right position of woman in the State is another index. Poverty and industry with a healthy mind read very easily the laws of humanity, and love them : place the sexes in right relations of mutual respect, and a severe morality gives that essential charm to woman which educates all that is delicate, poetic, and self - sacrificing ; breeds courtesy and learning, conversation and wit, in her rough mate ; so that I have thought a sufficient measure of civilization is the influence of good women.

[1] Dr. Thomas Brown.

Another measure of culture is the diffusion of knowledge, overrunning all the old barriers of caste, and, by the cheap press, bringing the university to every poor man's door in the newsboy's basket. Scraps of science, of thought, of poetry are in the coarsest sheet, so that in every house we hesitate to burn a newspaper until we have looked it through.

The ship, in its latest complete equipment, is an abridgment and compend of a nation's arts: the ship steered by compass and chart, longitude reckoned by lunar observation and by chronometer, driven by steam; and in wildest sea-mountains, at vast distances from home,

> " The pulses of her iron heart
> Go beating through the storm."

No use can lessen the wonder of this control by so weak a creature of forces so prodigious. I remember I watched, in crossing the sea, the beautiful skill whereby the engine in its constant working was made to produce two hundred gallons of fresh water out of salt water, every hour, — thereby supplying all the ship's want.

The skill that pervades complex details; the man that maintains himself; the chimney taught to burn its own smoke; the farm made to produce all that is consumed on it; the very prison compelled to maintain itself and yield a revenue, and, better still, made a reform school and a manufactory of honest men out of rogues, as the steamer made fresh water out of salt, — all these are examples of that tendency to combine antagonisms and utilize evil which is the index of high civilization.

Civilization is the result of highly complex organization. In the snake, all the organs are sheathed; no hands, no feet, no fins, no wings. In bird and beast the organs are released and begin to play. In man they are all unbound and full of joyful action. With this unswaddling he receives the absolute illumination we call Reason, and thereby true liberty.

Climate has much to do with this melioration. The highest civility has never loved the hot zones. Wherever snow falls there is usually civil freedom. Where the banana grows the animal system is indolent and pampered at the cost of higher qualities: the man is sensual and cruel. But this scale is not invariable. High degrees of moral sentiment control the unfavorable influences of climate; and some of our grandest examples of men and of races come from the equatorial regions, — as the genius of Egypt, of India, and of Arabia.

These feats are measures or traits of civility; and temperate climate is an important influence,

though not quite indispensable, for there have been
learning, philosophy and art in Iceland, and in the
tropics. But one condition is essential to the social
education of man, namely, morality. There can
be no high civility without a deep morality, though
it may not always call itself by that name, but
sometimes the point of honor, as in the institution
of chivalry; or patriotism, as in the Spartan and
Roman republics; or the enthusiasm of some religious sect which imputes its virtue to its dogma; or
the cabalism or *esprit de corps* of a masonic or
other association of friends.

The evolution of a highly-destined society must
be moral; it must run in the grooves of the celestial wheels. It must be catholic in aims. What
is *moral?* It is the respecting in action catholic
or universal ends. Hear the definition which Kant
gives of moral conduct: " Act always so that the
immediate motive of thy will may become a universal rule for all intelligent beings."

Civilization depends on morality. Everything
good in man leans on what is higher. This rule
holds in small as in great. Thus all our strength
and success in the work of our hands depend on
our borrowing the aid of the elements. You have
seen a carpenter on a ladder with a broad-axe chop-
ping upward chips from a beam. How awkward!
at what disadvantage he works! But see him on

the ground, dressing his timber under him. Now, not his feeble muscles but the force of gravity brings down the axe; that is to say, the planet itself splits his stick. The farmer had much ill-temper, laziness and shirking to endure from his hand-sawyers, until one day he bethought him to put his saw-mill on the edge of a waterfall; and the river never tires of turning his wheel; the river is good natured, and never hints an objection.

We had letters to send: couriers could not go fast enough nor far enough; broke their wagons, foundered their horses; bad roads in spring, snow-drifts in winter, heats in summer; could not get the horses out of a walk. But we found out that the air and earth were full of Electricity, and always going our way, — just the way we wanted to send. *Would he take a message?* Just as lief as not; had nothing else to do; would carry it in no time. Only one doubt occurred, one staggering objection, — he had no carpet-bag, no visible pockets, no hands, not so much as a mouth, to carry a letter. But after much thought and many experiments we managed to meet the conditions, and to fold up the letter in such invisible compact form as he could carry in those invisible pockets of his, never wrought by needle and thread, — and it went like a charm.

I admire still more than the saw-mill the skill

which, on the sea-shore, makes the tides drive the wheels and grind corn, and which thus engages the assistance of the moon, like a hired hand, to grind, and wind, and pump, and saw, and split stone, and roll iron.

Now that is the wisdom of a man, in every instance of his labor, to hitch his wagon to a star, and see his chore done by the gods themselves. That is the way we are strong, by borrowing the might of the elements. The forces of steam, gravity, galvanism, light, magnets, wind, fire, serve us day by day and cost us nothing.

Our astronomy is full of examples of calling in the aid of these magnificent helpers. Thus, on a planet so small as ours, the want of an adequate base for astronomical measurements is early felt, as, for example, in detecting the parallax of a star. But the astronomer, having by an observation fixed the place of a star, — by so simple an expedient as waiting six months and then repeating his observation, contrived to put the diameter of the earth's orbit, say two hundred millions of miles, between his first observation and his second, and this line afforded him a respectable base for his triangle.

All our arts aim to win this vantage. We cannot bring the heavenly powers to us, but if we will only choose our jobs in directions in which they travel, they will undertake them with the greatest pleasure. It is a peremptory rule with them that *they never go out of their road.* We are dapper little busybodies and run this way and that way superserviceably; but they swerve never from their foreordained paths, — neither the sun, nor the moon, nor a bubble of air, nor a mote of dust.

And as our handiworks borrow the elements, so all our social and political action leans on principles. To accomplish anything excellent the will must work for catholic and universal ends. A puny creature, walled in on every side, as Daniel wrote, —

> " Unless above himself he can
> Erect himself, how poor a thing is man ! "

but when his will leans on a principle, when he is the vehicle of ideas, he borrows their omnipotence. Gibraltar may be strong, but ideas are impregnable, and bestow on the hero their invincibility. " It was a great instruction," said a saint in Cromwell's war, " that the best courages are but beams of the Almighty." Hitch your wagon to a star. Let us not fag in paltry works which serve our pot and bag alone. Let us not lie and steal. No god will help. We shall find all their teams going the other way, — Charles's Wain, Great Bear, Orion, Leo, Hercules: every god will leave us. Work rather for those interests which the divinities honor and promote, — justice, love, freedom, knowledge, utility.

If we can thus ride in Olympian chariots by putting our works in the path of the celestial circuits, we can harness also evil agents, the powers of darkness, and force them to serve against their will the ends of wisdom and virtue. Thus a wise government puts fines and penalties on pleasant vices. What a benefit would the American government, not yet relieved of its extreme need, render to itself and to every city, village, and hamlet in the States, if it would tax whiskey and rum almost to the point of prohibition! Was it Bonaparte who said that he found vices very good patriots? — "he got five millions from the love of brandy, and he should be glad to know which of the virtues would pay him as much." Tobacco and opium have broad backs, and will cheerfully carry the load of armies, if you choose to make them pay high for such joy as they give and such harm as they do.

These are traits and measures and modes; and the true test of civilization is, not the census, nor the size of cities, nor the crops, — no, but the kind of man the country turns out. I see the vast advantages of this country, spanning the breadth of the temperate zone. I see the immense material prosperity, — towns on towns, states on states, and wealth piled in the massive architecture of cities;

California quartz-mountains dumped down in New York to be repiled architecturally along-shore from Canada to Cuba, and thence westward to California again. But it is not New York streets, built by the confluence of workmen and wealth of all nations, though stretching out towards Philadelphia until they touch it, and northward until they touch New Haven, Hartford, Springfield, Worcester, and Boston, — not these that make the real estimation. But when I look over this constellation of cities which animate and illustrate the land, and see how little the government has to do with their daily life, how self-helped and self-directed all families are, — knots of men in purely natural societies, societies of trade, of kindred blood, of habitual hospitality, house and house, man acting on man by weight of opinion, of longer or better-directed industry; the refining influence of women, the invitation which experience and permanent causes open to youth and labor : — when I see how much each virtuous and gifted person, whom all men consider, lives affectionately with scores of excellent people who are not known far from home, and perhaps with great reason reckons these people his superiors in virtue and in the symmetry and force of their qualities, — I see what cubic values America has, and in these a better certificate of civilization than great cities or enormous wealth.

In strictness, the vital refinements are the moral and intellectual steps. The appearance of the Hebrew Moses, of the Indian Buddh; in Greece, of the Seven Wise Masters, of the acute and upright Socrates, and of the stoic Zeno; in Judæa, the advent of Jesus, and, in modern Christendom, of the realists Huss, Savonarola, and Luther, — are causal facts which carry forward races to new convictions and elevate the rule of life. In the presence of these agencies it is frivolous to insist on the invention of printing or gunpowder, of steam-power or gas-light, percussion-caps and rubber-shoes, which are toys thrown off from that security, freedom, and exhilaration which a healthy morality creates in society. These arts add a comfort and smoothness to house and street life; but a purer morality, which kindles genius, civilizes civilization, casts backward all that we held sacred into the profane, as the flame of oil throws a shadow when shined upon by the flame of the Bude-light. Not the less the popular measures of progress will ever be the arts and the laws.

But if there be a country which cannot stand any one of these tests, — a country where knowledge cannot be diffused without perils of mob-law and statute-law; where speech is not free; where the post-office is violated, mail-bags opened, and letters tampered with; where public debts and private debts outside of the State are repudiated; where liberty is attacked in the primary institution of social life; where the position of the white woman is injuriously affected by the outlawry of the black woman; where the arts, such as they have, are all imported, having no indigenous life; where the laborer is not secured in the earnings of his own hands; where suffrage is not free or equal; — that country is, in all these respects, not civil, but barbarous; and no advantages of soil, climate, or coast can resist these suicidal mischiefs.

Morality and all the incidents of morality are essential; as, justice to the citizen, and personal liberty. Montesquieu says: " Countries are well cultivated, not as they are fertile, but as they are free;" and the remark holds not less but more true of the culture of men, than of the tillage of land. And the highest proof of civility is that the whole public action of the State is directed on securing the greatest good of the greatest number.

ART.

ART.

ALL departments of life at the present day, — Trade, Politics, Letters, Science, or Religion, — seem to feel, and to labor to express, the identity of their law. They are rays of one sun; they translate each into a new language the sense of the other. They are sublime when seen as emanations of a Necessity contradistinguished from the vulgar Fate by being instant and alive, and dissolving man as well as his works in its flowing beneficence. This influence is conspicuously visible in the principles and history of Art.

On one side in primary communication with absolute truth through thought and instinct, the human mind on the other side tends, by an equal necessity, to the publication and embodiment of its thought, modified and dwarfed by the impurity and untruth which in all our experience injure the individuality through which it passes. The child not only suffers, but cries; not only hungers, but eats. The man not only thinks, but speaks and acts. Every thought that arises in the mind, in its rising aims to pass out of the mind into act;

just as every plant, in the moment of germination,
struggles up to light. Thought is the seed of action; but action is as much its second form as
thought is its first. It rises in thought, to the end
that it may be uttered and acted. The more profound the thought, the more burdensome. Always
in proportion to the depth of its sense does it knock
importunately at the gates of the soul, to be spoken,
to be done. What is in, will out. It struggles to
the birth. Speech is a great pleasure, and action a
great pleasure; they cannot be foreborne.

The utterance of thought and emotion in speech
and action may be conscious or unconscious. The
sucking child is an unconscious actor. The man in
an ecstasy of fear or anger is an unconscious actor.
A large part of our habitual actions are unconsciously done, and most of our necessary words
are unconsciously said.

The conscious utterance of thought, by speech
or action, to any end, is Art. From the first imitative babble of a child to the despotism of eloquence; from his first pile of toys or chip bridge
to the masonry of Minot Rock Lighthouse or the
Pacific Railroad; from the tattooing of the Owhy-
hees to the Vatican Gallery; from the simplest expedient of private prudence to the American Constitution; from its first to its last works, Art is the
spirit's voluntary use and combination of things to

serve its end. The Will distinguishes it as spiritual action. Relatively to themselves, the bee, the
bird, the beaver, have no art; for what they do
they do instinctively; but relatively to the Supreme
Being, they have. And the same is true of all
unconscious action: relatively to the doer, it is instinct; relatively to the First Cause, it is Art. In
this sense, recognizing the Spirit which informs
Nature, Plato rightly said, "Those things which
are said to be done by Nature are indeed done by
Divine Art." Art, universally, is the spirit creative. It was defined by Aristotle, "The reason of
the thing, without the matter."

If we follow the popular distinction of works
according to their aim, we should say, the Spirit,
in its creation, aims at use or at beauty, and hence
Art divides itself into the Useful and the Fine Arts.

The useful arts comprehend not only those that
lie next to instinct, as agriculture, building, weaving, &c., but also navigation, practical chemistry,
and the construction of all the grand and delicate
tools and instruments by which man serves himself;
as language, the watch, the ship, the decimal cipher; and also the sciences, so far as they are
made serviceable to political economy.

When we reflect on the pleasure we receive from
a ship, a railroad, a dry-dock; or from a picture, a
dramatic representation, a statue, a poem, — we find

that these have not a quite simple, but a blended
origin. We find that the question, What is Art?
leads us directly to another, — Who is the Artist?
And the solution of this is the key to the history of
Art.

I hasten to state the principle which prescribes,
through different means, its firm law to the useful
and the beautiful arts. The law is this. The universal soul is the alone creator of the useful and
the beautiful ; therefore to make anything useful or
beautiful, the individual must be submitted to the
universal mind.

In the first place let us consider this in reference
to the useful arts. Here the omnipotent agent is
Nature ; all human acts are satellites to her orb.
Nature is the representative of the universal mind,
and the law becomes this, — that Art must be a
complement to nature, strictly subsidiary. It was
said, in allusion to the great structures of the
ancient Romans, the aqueducts and bridges, that
"their Art was a Nature working to municipal
ends." That is a true account of all just works
of useful art. Smeaton built Eddystone Lighthouse on the model of an oak-tree, as being the
form in nature best designed to resist a constant
assailing force. Dollond formed his achromatic
telescope on the model of the human eye. Duhamel
built a bridge by letting in a piece of stronger tim-

ber for the middle of the under surface, getting his
hint from the structure of the shin-bone.

The first and last lesson of the useful arts is that
Nature tyrannizes over our works. They must be
conformed to her law, or they will be ground to
powder by her omnipresent activity. Nothing droll,
nothing whimsical will endure. Nature is ever in-
terfering with Art. You cannot build your house
or pagoda as you will, but as you must. There is
a quick bound set to your caprice. The leaning
tower can only lean so far. The verandah or pagoda roof can curve upward only to a certain point.
The slope of your roof is determined by the weight
of snow. It is only within narrow limits that the
discretion of the architect may range : gravity,
wind, sun, rain, the size of men and animals, and
such like, have more to say than he. It is the law
of fluids that prescribes the shape of the boat, —
keel, rudder, and bows, — and, in the finer fluid
above, the form and tackle of the sails. Man seems
to have no option about his tools, but merely the
necessity to learn from Nature what will fit best,
as if he were fitting a screw or a door. Beneath a
necessity thus almighty, what is artificial in man's
life seems insignificant. He seems to take his task
so minutely from intimations of Nature, that his
works become as it were hers, and he is no longer
free.

But if we work within this limit, she yields us all her strength. All powerful action is performed by bringing the forces of nature to bear upon our objects. We do not grind corn or lift the loom by our own strength, but we build a mill in such position as to set the north wind to play upon our instrument, or the elastic force of steam, or the ebb and flow of the sea. So in our handiwork, we do few things by muscular force, but we place ourselves in such attitudes as to bring the force of gravity, that is, the weight of the planet, to bear upon the spade or the axe we wield. In short, in all our operations we seek not to use our own, but to bring a quite infinite force to bear.

Let us now consider this law as it affects the works that have beauty for their end, that is, the productions of the Fine Arts. Here again the prominent fact is subordination of man. His art is the least part of his work of art. A great deduction is to be made before we can know his proper contribution to it.

Music, Eloquence, Poetry, Painting, Sculpture, Architecture. This is a rough enumeration of the Fine Arts. I omit Rhetoric, which only respects the form of eloquence and poetry. Architecture and eloquence are mixed arts, whose end is sometimes beauty and sometimes use.

It will be seen that in each of these arts there is

much which is not spiritual. Each has a material
basis, and in each the creating intellect is crippled
in some degree by the stuff on which it works.
The basis of poetry is language, which is material
only on one side. It is a demi-god. But being
applied primarily to the common necessities of
man, it is not new-created by the poet for his own
ends.

The basis of music is the qualities of the air and
the vibrations of sonorous bodies. The pulsation
of a stretched string or wire gives the ear the pleasure of sweet sound, before yet the musician has
enhanced this pleasure by concords and combinations.

Eloquence, as far as it is a fine art, is modified
how much by the material organization of the orator, the tone of the voice, the physical strength, the
play of the eye and countenance. All this is so
much deduction from the purely spiritual pleasure,
as so much deduction from the merit of Art, and
is the attribute of Nature.

In painting, bright colors stimulate the eye before yet they are harmonized into a landscape. In
sculpture and in architecture the material, as marble or granite, and in architecture the mass, are
sources of great pleasure quite independent of the
artificial arrangement. The art resides in the
model, in the plan; for it is on that the genius of

the artist is expended, not on the statue or the temple. Just as much better as is the polished statue of dazzling marble than the clay model, or as much more impressive as is the granite cathedral or pyramid than the ground-plan or profile of them on paper, so much more beauty owe they to Nature than to Art.

There is a still larger deduction to be made from the genius of the artist in favor of Nature than I have yet specified.

A jumble of musical sounds on a viol or a flute, in which the rhythm of the tune is played without one of the notes being right, gives pleasure to the unskilful ear. A very coarse imitation of the human form on canvas, or in wax-work; a coarse sketch in colors of a landscape, in which imitation is all that is attempted, — these things give to unpractised eyes, to the uncultured, who do not ask a fine spiritual delight, almost as much pleasure as a statue of Canova or a picture of Titian. And in the statue of Canova or the picture of Titian, these give the great part of the pleasure; they are the basis on which the fine spirit rears a higher delight, but to which these are indispensable.

Another deduction from the genius of the artist is what is conventional in his art, of which there is much in every work of art. Thus how much is there that is not original in every particular build-

ing, in every statue, in every tune, painting, poem,
or harangue ! — whatever is national or usual ; as
the usage of building all Roman churches in the
form of a cross, the prescribed distribution of parts
of a theatre, the custom of draping a statue in
classical costume. Yet who will deny that the
merely conventional part of the performance con-
tributes much to its effect ?

One consideration more exhausts I believe all
the deductions from the genius of the artist in any
given work. This is the adventitious. Thus the
pleasure that a noble temple gives us is only in
part owing to the temple. It is exalted by the
beauty of sunlight, the play of the clouds, the landscape around it, its grouping with the houses, trees,
and towers in its vicinity. The pleasure of eloquence is in greatest part owing often to the stim-
ulus of the occasion which produces it, — to the
magic of sympathy, which exalts the feeling of
each by radiating on him the feeling of all.

The effect of music belongs how much to the
place, as the church, or the moonlight walk ; or to
the company ; or, if on the stage, to what went before in the play, or to the expectation of what shall
come after.

In poetry, " It is tradition more than invention
that helps the poet to a good fable." The adventitious beauty of poetry may be felt in the greater

delight which a verse gives in happy quotation than
in the poem.

It is a curious proof of our conviction that the
artist does not feel himself to be the parent of his
work, and is as much surprised at the effect as we,
that we are so unwilling to impute our best sense of
any work of art to the author. The highest praise
we can attribute to any writer, painter, sculptor,
builder, is, that he actually possessed the thought
or feeling with which he has inspired us. We hesitate at doing Spenser so great an honor as to
think that he intended by his allegory the sense we
affix to it. We grudge to Homer the wide human
circumspection his commentators ascribe to him.

Even Shakspeare, of whom we can believe every
thing, we think indebted to Goethe and to Coleridge for the wisdom they detect in his Hamlet and
Antony. Especially have we this infirmity of faith
in contemporary genius. We fear that Allston
and Greenough did not foresee and design all the
effect they produce on us. Our arts are happy
hits. We are like the musician on the lake, whose
melody is sweeter than he knows, or like a traveller surprised by a mountain echo, whose trivial
word returns to him in romantic thunders.

In view of these facts, I say that the power of
Nature predominates over the human will in all
works of even the fine arts, in all that respects

their material and external circumstances. Nature paints the best part of the picture, carves the best part of the statue, builds the best part of the house, and speaks the best part of the oration. For all the advantages to which I have adverted are such as the artist did not consciously produce. He relied on their aid, he put himself in the way to receive aid from some of them; but he saw that his planting and his watering waited for the sunlight of Nature, or were vain.

Let us proceed to the consideration of the law stated in the beginning of this essay, as it affects the purely spiritual part of a work of art.

As, in useful art, so far as it is useful, the work must be strictly subordinated to the laws of Nature, so as to become a sort of continuation and in no wise a contradiction of Nature; so in art that aims at beauty must the parts be subordinated to Ideal Nature, and everything individual abstracted, so that it shall be the production of the universal soul. The artist who is to produce a work which is to be admired, not by his friends or his townspeople or his contemporaries but by all men, and which is to be more beautiful to the eye in proportion to its culture, must disindividualize himself, and be a man of no party and no manner and no age, but one through whom the soul of all men circulates as the common air through his lungs. He must work in the spirit in which we conceive a prophet to speak, or an angel of the Lord to act; that is, he is not to speak his own words, or do his own works, or think his own thoughts, but he is to be an organ through which the universal mind acts.

In speaking of the useful arts, I pointed to the fact that we do not dig, or grind, or hew, by our muscular strength, but by bringing the weight of the planet to bear on the spade, axe, or bar. Precisely analogous to this, in the fine arts, is the manner of our intellectual work. We aim to hinder our individuality from acting. So much as we can shove aside our egotism, our prejudice and will, and bring the omniscience of reason upon the subject before us, so perfect is the work. The wonders of Shakspeare are things which he saw whilst he stood aside, and then returned to record them. The poet aims at getting observations without aim; to subject to thought things seen without (voluntary) thought.

In eloquence, the great triumphs of the art are when the orator is lifted above himself; when consciously he makes himself the mere tongue of the occasion and the hour, and says what cannot but be said. Hence the term *abandonment*, to describe the self-surrender of the orator. Not his will, but the principle on which he is horsed, the great con-

nection and crisis of events, thunder in the ear of
the crowd.

In poetry, where every word is free, every word
is necessary. Good poetry could not have been
otherwise written than it is. The first time you
hear it, it sounds rather as if copied out of some
invisible tablet in the Eternal mind, than as if ar-
bitrarily composed by the poet. The feeling of all
great poets has accorded with this. They found
the verse, not made it. The muse brought it to
them.

In sculpture, did ever anybody call the Apollo a
fancy piece? Or say of the Laocoön how it might
be made different? A masterpiece of art has in the
mind a fixed place in the chain of being, as much
as a plant or a crystal.

The whole language of men, especially of artists,
in reference to this subject, points at the belief
that every work of art, in proportion to its excellence, partakes of the precision of fate: no room
was there for choice, no play for fancy; for in the
moment or in the successive moments when that
form was seen, the iron lids of Reason were un-
closed, which ordinarily are heavy with slumber.
The individual mind became for the moment the
vent of the mind of humanity.

There is but one Reason. The mind that made
the world is not one mind, but *the* mind. And

every work of art is a more or less pure manifestation of the same. Therefore we arrive at this conclusion, which I offer as a confirmation of the whole
view, that the delight which a work of art affords,
seems to arise from our recognizing in it the mind
that formed Nature, again in active operation. It
differs from the works of Nature in this, that they
are organically reproductive. This is not, but
spiritually it is prolific by its powerful action on
the intellects of men.

Hence it follows that a study of admirable works
of art sharpens our perceptions of the beauty of
Nature; that a certain analogy reigns throughout
the wonders of both; that the contemplation of a
work of great art draws us into a state of mind
which may be called religious. It conspires with
all exalted sentiments.

Proceeding from absolute mind, whose nature is
goodness as much as truth, the great works are
always attuned to moral nature. If the earth and
sea conspire with virtue more than vice, — so do the
masterpieces of art. The galleries of ancient sculpture in Naples and Rome strike no deeper conviction into the mind than the contrast of the purity,
the severity expressed in these fine old heads, with
the frivolity and grossness of the mob that exhibits
and the mob that gazes at them. These are the
countenances of the first-born, — the face of man

in the morning of the world. No mark is on these lofty features of sloth, or luxury, or meanness, and they surprise you with a moral admonition, as they speak of nothing around you, but remind you of the fragrant thoughts and the purest resolutions of your youth.

Herein is the explanation of the analogies which exist in all the arts. They are the reappearance of one mind, working in many materials to many temporary ends. Raphael paints wisdom, Handel sings it, Phidias carves it, Shakspeare writes it, Wren builds it, Columbus sails it, Luther preaches it, Washington arms it, Watt mechanizes it. Painting was called " silent poetry," and poetry "speaking painting." The laws of each art are convertible into the laws of every other.

Herein we have an explanation of the necessity that reigns in all the kingdom of Art. Arising out of eternal Reason, one and perfect, whatever is beautiful rests on the foundation of the necessary. Nothing is arbitrary, nothing is insulated in beauty. It depends forever on the necessary and the useful. The plumage of the bird, the mimic plumage of the insect, has a reason for its rich colors in the constitution of the animal. Fitness is so inseparable an accompaniment of beauty, that it has been taken for it. The most perfect form to answer an end is so far beautiful. We feel, in seeing a noble building,

which rhymes well, as we do in hearing a perfect
song, that it is spiritually organic ; that is, had a
necessity, in nature, for being ; was one of the possible forms in the Divine mind, and is now only
discovered and executed by the artist, not arbitra-
rily composed by him.

And so every genuine work of art has as much
reason for being as the earth and the sun. The
gayest charm of beauty has a root in the constitution of things. The Iliad of Homer, the songs of
David, the odes of Pindar, the tragedies of Æschylus, the Doric temples, the Gothic cathedrals, the
plays of Shakspeare, all and each were made not
for sport but in grave earnest, in tears and smiles
of suffering and loving men.

Viewed from this point the history of Art becomes intelligible, and moreover one of the most
agreeable studies. We see how each work of art
sprang irresistibly from necessity, and, moreover,
took its form from the broad hint of Nature. Beautiful in this wise is the obvious origin of all the
known orders of architecture ; namely, that they
were the idealizing of the primitive abodes of each
people. There was no wilfulness in the savages in
this perpetuating of their first rude abodes. The
first form in which they built a house would be the
first form of their public and religious edifice also.
This form becomes immediately sacred in the eyes

of their children, and as more traditions cluster round it, is imitated with more splendor in each succeeding generation.

In like manner it has been remarked by Goethe that the granite breaks into parallelopipeds, which broken in two, one part would be an obelisk; that in Upper Egypt the inhabitants would naturally mark a memorable spot by setting up so conspicuous a stone. Again, he suggested, we may see in any stone wall, on a fragment of rock, the projecting veins of harder stone which have resisted the action of frost and water which has decomposed the rest. This appearance certainly gave the hint of the hieroglyphics inscribed on their obelisk. The amphitheatre of the old Romans, — any one may see its origin who looks at the crowd running together to see any fight, sickness, or odd appearance in the street. The first comers gather round in a circle, those behind stand on tiptoe, and farther back they climb on fences or window-sills, and so make a cup of which the object of attention occupies the hollow area. The architect put benches in this, and enclosed the cup with a wall, — and behold a Coliseum!

It would be easy to show of many fine things in the world, — in the customs of nations, the etiquette of courts, the constitution of governments, — the origin in quite simple local necessities. Heraldry

for example, and the ceremonies of a coronation, are
a dignified repetition of the occurrences that might
befall a dragoon and his footboy. The College
of Cardinals were originally the parish priests of
Rome. The leaning towers originated from the
civil discords which induced every lord to build a
tower. Then it became a point of family pride, —
and for more pride the novelty of a leaning tower
was built.

This strict dependence of Art upon material and
ideal Nature, this adamantine necessity which un-
derlies it, has made all its past and may foreshow
its future history. It never was in the power of
any man or any community to call the arts into
being. They come to serve his actual wants, never
to please his fancy. These arts have their origin
always in some enthusiasm, as love, patriotism,
or religion. Who carved marble? The believing
man, who wished to symbolize their gods to the
waiting Greeks.

The Gothic cathedrals were built when the
builder and the priest and the people were overpowered by their faith. Love and fear laid every
stone. The Madonnas of Raphael and Titian were
made to be worshipped. Tragedy was instituted
for the like purpose, and the miracles of music : all
sprang out of some genuine enthusiasm, and never
out of dilettanteism and holidays. Now they lan-

guish, because their purpose is merely exhibition.
Who cares, who knows what works of art our government have ordered to be made for the Capitol?
They are a mere flourish to please the eye of persons who have associations with books and galleries. But in Greece, the Demos of Athens divided
into political factions upon the merits of Phidias.

In this country, at this time, other interests than
religion and patriotism are predominant, and the
arts, the daughters of enthusiasm, do not flourish.
The genuine offspring of our ruling passions we
behold. Popular institutions, the school, the read-
ing-room, the telegraph, the post-office, the exchange, the insurance-company, and the immense
harvest of economical inventions, are the fruit of
the equality and the boundless liberty of lucrative
callings. These are superficial wants; and their
fruits are these superficial institutions. But, as far
as they accelerate the end of political freedom and
national education, they are preparing the soil of
man for fairer flowers and fruits in another age.
For beauty, truth, and goodness are not obsolete;
they spring eternal in the breast of man; they are
as indigenous in Massachusetts as in Tuscany or
the Isles of Greece. And that Eternal Spirit whose
triple face they are, moulds from them forever, for
his mortal child, images to remind him of the Infinite and Fair.

ELOQUENCE.

.

ELOQUENCE.

It is the doctrine of the popular music-masters that whoever can speak can sing. So probably every man is eloquent once in his life. Our temperaments differ in capacity of heat, or, we boil at different degrees. One man is brought to the boiling-point by the excitement of conversation in the parlor. The waters, of course, are not very deep. He has a two-inch enthusiasm, a patty-pan ebullition. Another requires the additional caloric of a multitude and a public debate; a third needs an antagonist, or a hot indignation; a fourth needs a revolution; and a fifth, nothing less than the grandeur of absolute ideas, the splendors and shades of Heaven and Hell.

But, because every man is an orator, how long soever he may have been a mute, an assembly of men is so much more susceptible. The eloquence of one stimulates all the rest, some up to the speaking-point and all others to a degree that makes them good receivers and conductors, and they avenge themselves for their enforced silence by increased loquacity on their return to the fireside.

The plight of these phlegmatic brains is better than that of those who prematurely boil, and who impatiently break silence before their time. Our county conventions often exhibit a small-pot-soon-hot style of eloquence. We are too much reminded of a medical experiment where a series of patients are taking nitrous-oxide gas. Each patient in turn exhibits similar symptoms, — redness in the face, volubility, violent gesticulation, delirious attitudes, occasional stamping, an alarming loss of perception of the passage of time, a selfish enjoyment of his sensations, and loss of perception of the sufferings of the audience.

Plato says that the punishment which the wise suffer who refuse to take part in the government, is, to live under the government of worse men; and the like regret is suggested to all the auditors, as the penalty of abstaining to speak, — that they shall hear worse orators than themselves.

But this lust to speak marks the universal feeling of the energy of the engine, and the curiosity men feel to touch the springs. Of all the musical instruments on which men play, a popular assembly is that which has the largest compass and variety, and out of which, by genius and study, the most wonderful effects can be drawn. An audience is not a simple addition of the individuals that compose it. Their sympathy gives them a certain so-

cial organism, which fills each member, in his own
degree, and most of all the orator, as a jar in a
battery is charged with the whole electricity of the
battery. No one can survey the face of an excited
assembly, without being apprised of new opportunity for painting in fire human thought, and being
agitated to agitate. How many orators sit mute
there below! They come to get justice done to
that ear and intuition which no Chatham and no
Demosthenes has begun to satisfy.

The Welsh Triads say, "Many are the friends of
the golden tongue." Who can wonder at the at-
tractiveness of Parliament, or of Congress, or the
bar, for our ambitious young men, when the highest
bribes of society are at the feet of the successful
orator? He has his audience at his devotion. All
other fames must hush before his. He is the true
potentate; for they are not kings who sit on thrones,
but they who know how to govern. The definitions
of eloquence describe its attraction for young men.
Antiphon the Rhamnusian, one of Plutarch's ten
orators, advertised in Athens "that he would cure
distempers of the mind with words." No man has
a prosperity so high or firm but two or three words
can dishearten it. There is no calamity which
right words will not begin to redress. Isocrates
described his art as "the power of magnifying
what was small and diminishing what was great,"

— an acute but partial definition. Among the Spartans, the art assumed a Spartan shape, namely, of the sharpest weapon. Socrates says: " If any one wishes to converse with the meanest of the Lacedæmonians, he will at first find him despicable in conversation, but when a proper opportunity offers, this same person, like a skilful jaculator, will hurl a sentence worthy of attention, short and contorted, so that he who converses with him will appear to be in no respect superior to a boy." Plato's definition of rhetoric is, " the art of ruling the minds of men." The Koran says, " A mountain may change its place, but a man will not change his disposition ; " yet the end of eloquence is, — is it not ? — to alter in a pair of hours, perhaps in a half-hour's discourse, the convictions and habits of years. Young men, too, are eager to enjoy this sense of added power and enlarged sympathetic existence. The orator sees himself the organ of a multitude, and concentrating their valors and powers : —

> " But now the blood of twenty thousand men
>   Blushed in my face."

That which he wishes, that which eloquence ought to reach, is not a particular skill in telling a story, or neatly summing up evidence, or arguing logically, or dexterously addressing the prejudice of the company, — no, but a taking sovereign possession of the audience. Him we call an artist who shall play on an assembly of men as a master on the keys of the piano, — who, seeing the people furious, shall soften and compose them, shall draw them, when he will, to laughter and to tears. Bring him to his audience, and, be they who they may, — coarse or refined, pleased or displeased, sulky or savage, with their opinions in the keeping of a confessor, or with their opinions in their bank-safes, — he will have them pleased and humored as he chooses; and they shall carry and execute that which he bids them.

This is that despotism which poets have celebrated in the "Pied Piper of Hamelin," whose music drew like the power of gravitation, — drew soldiers and priests, traders and feasters, women and boys, rats and mice; or that of the minstrel of Meudon, who made the pall-bearers dance around the bier. This is a power of many degrees and requiring in the orator a great range of faculty and experience, requiring a large composite man, such as Nature rarely organizes; so that in our experience we are forced to gather up the figure in fragments, here one talent and there another.

The audience is a constant meter of the orator. There are many audiences in every public assembly, each one of which rules in turn. If anything comic and coarse is spoken, you shall see the emergence

of the boys and rowdies, so loud and vivacious that
you might think the house was filled with them.
If new topics are started, graver and higher, these
roisters recede; a more chaste and wise attention
takes place. You would think the boys slept, and
that the men have any degree of profoundness. If
the speaker utter a noble sentiment, the attention
deepens, a new and highest audience now listens,
and the audiences of the fun and of facts and
of the understanding are all silenced and awed.
There is also something excellent in every audience, — the capacity of virtue. They are ready to
be beatified. They know so much more than the
orator, — and are so just! There is a tablet there
for every line he can inscribe, though he should
mount to the highest levels. Humble persons are
conscious of new illumination; narrow brows ex-
pand with enlarged affections; — delicate spirits,
long unknown to themselves, masked and muffled
in coarsest fortunes, who now hear their own native
language for the first time, and leap to hear it.
But all these several audiences, each above each,
which successively appear to greet the variety of
style and topic, are really composed out of the
same persons; nay, sometimes the same individual
will take active part in them all, in turn.

This range of many powers in the consummate
speaker, and of many audiences in one assembly,
leads us to consider the successive stages of oratory.

Perhaps it is the lowest of the qualities of an orator, but it is, on so many occasions, of chief importance, — a certain robust and radiant physical health; or, — shall I say? — great volumes of animal heat. When each auditor feels himself to make too large a part of the assembly, and shudders with cold at the thinness of the morning audience, and with fear lest all will heavily fail through one bad speech, mere energy and mellowness are then inestimable. Wisdom and learning would be harsh and unwelcome, compared with a substantial cordial man, made of milk as we say, who is a house-warmer, with his obvious honesty and good meaning, and a hue-and-cry style of harangue, which inundates the assembly with a flood of animal spirits, and makes all safe and secure, so that any and every sort of good speaking becomes at once practicable. I do not rate this animal eloquence very highly; and yet, as we must be fed and warmed before we can do any work well, — even the best, — so is this semi-animal exuberance, like a good stove, of the first necessity in a cold house.

Climate has much to do with it, — climate and race. Set a New-Englander to describe any accident which happened in his presence. What hesitation and reserve in his narrative! He tells with difficulty some particulars, and gets as fast as he can to the result, and, though he cannot describe,

hopes to suggest the whole scene. Now listen to
a poor Irishwoman recounting some experience of
hers. Her speech flows like a river, — so uncon-
sidered, so humorous, so pathetic, such justice done
to all the parts! It is a true transubstantiation, —
the fact converted into speech, all warm and colored
and alive, as it fell out. Our Southern people are
almost all speakers, and have every advantage over
the New England people, whose climate is so cold
that 't is said we do not like to open our mouths
very wide. But neither can the Southerner in the
United States, nor the Irish, compare with the
lively inhabitant of the south of Europe. The
traveller in Sicily needs no gayer melodramatic
exhibition than the *table d'hôte* of his inn will afford him in the conversation of the joyous guests.
They mimic the voice and manner of the person
they describe; they crow, squeal, hiss, cackle, bark,
and scream like mad, and, were it only by the physical strength exerted in telling the story, keep the
table in unbounded excitement. But in every constitution some large degree of animal vigor is necessary as material foundation for the higher qualities
of the art.

But eloquence must be attractive, or it is none.
The virtue of books is to be readable, and of orators to be interesting; and this is a gift of Nature;
as Demosthenes, the most laborious student in that

kind, signified his sense of this necessity when he wrote, "Good Fortune," as his motto on his shield. As we know, the power of discourse of certain individuals amounts to fascination, though it may have no lasting effect. Some portion of this sugar must intermingle. The right eloquence needs no bell to call the people together, and no constable to keep them. It draws the children from their play, the old from their arm-chairs, the invalid from his warm chamber : it holds the hearer fast ; steals away his feet, that he shall not depart ; his memory, that he shall not remember the most pressing affairs ; his belief, that he shall not admit any opposing considerations. The pictures we have of it in semi-barbarous ages, when it has some advantages in the simpler habit of the people, show what it aims at. It is said that the Khans or story-tellers in Ispahan and other cities of the East, attain a controlling power over their audience, keeping them for many hours attentive to the most fanciful and extravagant adventures. The whole world knows pretty well the style of these improvisators, and how fascinating they are, in our translations of the "Arabian Nights." Scheherezade tells these stories to save her life, and the delight of young Europe and young America in them proves that she fairly earned it. And who does not remember in childhood some white or black or yellow Sche-

herezade, who, by that talent of telling endless feats
of fairies and magicians and kings and queens, was
more dear and wonderful to a circle of children
than any orator in England or America is now?
The more indolent and imaginative complexion of
the Eastern nations makes them much more im-
pressible by these appeals to the fancy.

These legends are only exaggerations of real occurrences, and every literature contains these high
compliments to the art of the orator and the bard,
from the Hebrew and the Greek down to the Scottish Glenkindie, who

> " harpit a fish out o' saut-water,
> Or water out of a stone,
> Or milk out of a maiden's breast
> Who bairn had never none."

Homer specially delighted in drawing the same
figure. For what is the Odyssey but a history
of the orator, in the largest style, carried through
a series of adventures furnishing brilliant oppor-
tunities to his talent? See with what care and
pleasure the poet brings him on the stage. Helen
is pointing out to Priam, from a tower, the different
Grecian chiefs. "The old man asked: 'Tell me,
dear child, who is that man, shorter by a head than
Agamemnon, yet he looks broader in his shoulders
and breast. His arms lie on the ground, but he,
like a leader, walks about the bands of the men.

He seems to me like a stately ram, who goes as
a master of the flock.' Him answered Helen,
daughter of Jove, 'This is the wise Ulysses, son
of Laertes, who was reared in the state of craggy
Ithaca, knowing all wiles and wise counsels.' To
her the prudent Antenor replied again : 'O woman,
you have spoken truly. For once the wise Ulysses
came hither on an embassy, with Menelaus, beloved
by Mars. I received them and entertained them at
my house. I became acquainted with the genius
and the prudent judgments of both. When they
mixed with the assembled Trojans, and stood,
the broad shoulders of Menalaus rose above the
other ; but, both sitting, Ulysses was more majestic.
When they conversed, and interweaved stories and
opinions with all, Menelaus spoke succinctly, — few
but very sweet words, since he was not talkative
nor superfluous in speech, and was the younger.
But when the wise Ulysses arose and stood and
looked down, fixing his eyes on the ground, and
neither moved his sceptre backward nor forward,
but held it still, like an awkward person, you would
say it was some angry or foolish man ; but when he
sent his great voice forth out of his breast, and his
words fell like the winter snows, not then would
any mortal contend with Ulysses ; and we, behold-
ing, wondered not afterwards so much at his aspect.' " [1]   Thus he does not fail to arm Ulysses at

[1] Iliad, III. 191.

first with this power of overcoming all opposition
by the blandishments of speech. Plutarch tells us
that Thucydides, when Archidamus, king of Sparta,
asked him which was the best wrestler, Pericles
or he, replied, " When I throw him, he says he
was never down, and he persuades the very spectators to believe him." Philip of Macedon said of
Demosthenes, on hearing the report of one of his
orations, " Had I been there, he would have per-
suaded me to take up arms against myself ; " and
Warren Hastings said of Burke's speech on his
impeachment, " As I listened to the orator, I felt
for more than half an hour as if I were the most
culpable being on earth."

In these examples, higher qualities have already
entered, but the power of detaining the ear by
pleasing speech, and addressing the fancy and imagination, often exists without higher merits. Thus
separated, as this fascination of discourse aims only
at amusement, though it be decisive in its momentary effect, it is yet a juggle, and of no lasting
power. It is heard like a band of music passing
through the streets, which converts all the passengers into poets, but is forgotten as soon as it has
turned the next corner ; and unless this oiled tongue
could, in Oriental phrase, lick the sun and moon
away, it must take its place with opium and
brandy. I know no remedy against it but cotton.

wool, or the wax which Ulysses stuffed into the ears of his sailors to pass the Sirens safely.

There are all degrees of power, and the least are interesting, but they must not be confounded. There is the glib tongue and cool self-possession of the salesman in a large shop, which, as is well known, overpower the prudence and resolution of housekeepers of both sexes. There is a petty lawyer's fluency, which is sufficiently impressive to him who is devoid of that talent, though it be, in so many cases, nothing more than a facility of expressing with accuracy and speed what everybody thinks and says more slowly; without new information, or precision of thought, but the same thing, neither less nor more. It requires no special insight to edit one of our country newspapers. Yet whoever can say off currently, sentence by sentence, matter neither better nor worse than what is there printed, will be very impressive to our easily pleased population. These talkers are of that class who prosper, like the celebrated schoolmaster, by being only one lesson ahead of the pupil. Add a little sarcasm and prompt allusion to passing occurrences, and you have the mischievous member of Congress. A spice of malice, a ruffian touch in his rhetoric, will do him no harm with his audience. These accomplishments are of the same kind, and only a degree higher than the coaxing of the auctioneer, or the vituperative style well described in the street-word "jawing." These kinds of public and private speaking have their use and convenience to the practitioners; but we may say of such collectively that the habit of oratory is apt to disqualify them for eloquence.

One of our statesmen said, "The curse of this country is eloquent men." And one cannot wonder at the uneasiness sometimes manifested by trained statesmen, with large experience of public affairs, when they observe the disproportionate advantage suddenly given to oratory over the most solid and accumulated public service. In a Senate or other business committee, the solid result depends on a few men with working-talent. They know how to deal with the facts before them, to put things into a practical shape, and they value men only as they can forward the work. But a new man comes there who has no capacity for helping them at all, is insignificant, and nobody in the committee, but has a talent for speaking. In the debate with open doors, this precious person makes a speech which is printed and read all over the Union, and he at once becomes famous, and takes the lead in the public mind over all these executive men, who, of course, are full of indignation to find one who has no tact or skill and knows he has none, put over them by means of this talking-power which they despise.

Leaving behind us these pretensions, better or worse, to come a little nearer to the verity, — eloquence is attractive as an example of the magic of personal ascendency, — a total and resultant power, rare, because it requires a rich coincidence of powers, intellect, will, sympathy, organs, and, over all, good fortune in the cause. We have a half-belief that the person is possible who can counterpoise all other persons. We believe that there may be a man who is a match for events, one who never found his match, against whom other men being dashed are broken, — one of inexhaustible personal resources, who can give you any odds and beat you. What we really wish for is a mind equal to any exigency. You are safe in your rural district, or in the city, in broad daylight, amidst the police, and under the eyes of a hundred thousand people. But how is it on the Atlantic, in a storm, — do you understand how to infuse your reason into men disabled by terror, and to bring yourself off safe then? — how among thieves, or among an infuriated populace, or among cannibals? Face to face with a highwayman who has every temptation and opportunity for violence and plunder, can you bring yourself off safe by your wit exercised through speech? — a problem easy enough to Cæsar or Napoleon. Whenever a man of that stamp arrives, the highwayman has found a master. What

a difference between men in power of face! A
man succeeds because he has more power of eye
than another, and so coaxes or confounds him.
The newspapers, every week, report the adventures
of some impudent swindler, who, by steadiness of
carriage, duped those who should have known better. Yet any swindlers we have known are novices
and bunglers, as is attested by their ill name. A
greater power of face would accomplish anything,
and, with the rest of their takings, take away the
bad name. A greater power of carrying the thing
loftily and with perfect assurance, would confound
merchant, banker, judge, men of influence and
power, poet and president, and might head any
party, unseat any sovereign, and abrogate any constitution in Europe and America. It was said that
a man has at one step attained vast power, who
has renounced his moral sentiment, and settled it
with himself that he will no longer stick at anything. It was said of Sir William Pepperel, one
of the worthies of New England, that, "put him
where you might, he commanded, and saw what he
willed come to pass." Julius Cæsar said to Metel-
lus, when that tribune interfered to hinder him
from entering the Roman treasury, "Young man,
it is easier for me to put you to death than to say
that I will;" and the youth yielded. In earlier
days, he was taken by pirates. What then? He

threw himself into their ship, established the most
extraordinary intimacies, told them stories, de-
claimed to them; if they did not applaud his
speeches, he threatened them with hanging, —
which he performed afterwards, — and, in a short
time, was master of all on board. A man this is
who cannot be disconcerted, and so can never play
his last card, but has a reserve of power when he
has hit his mark. With a serene face, he subverts
a kingdom. What is told of him is miraculous ;
it affects men so. The confidence of men in him
is lavish, and he changes the face of the world, and
histories, poems, and new philosophies arise to account for him. A supreme commander over all
his passions and affections ; but the secret of his
ruling is higher than that. It is the power of Nature running without impediment from the brain
and will into the hands. Men and women are his
game. Where they are, he cannot be without resource. " Whoso can speak well," said Luther,
" is a man." It was men of this stamp that the
Grecian States used to ask of Sparta for generals.
They did not send to Lacedæmon for troops, but
they said, " Send us a commander ; " and Pausa-
nias, or Gylippus, or Brasidas, or Agis, was de-
spatched by the Ephors.

It is easy to illustrate this overpowering personality by these examples of soldiers and kings ; but

there are men of the most peaceful way of life and
peaceful principle, who are felt wherever they go,
as sensibly as a July sun or a December frost, —
men who, if they speak, are heard, though they
speak in a whisper, — who, when they act, act effectually, and what they do is imitated; and these
examples may be found on very humble platforms
as well as on high ones.

In old countries a high money-value is set on
the services of men who have achieved a personal
distinction.   He who has points to carry must hire,
not a skilful attorney, but a commanding person. A
barrister in England is reputed to have made thirty
or forty thousand pounds *per annum* in representing the claims of railroad companies before commit-
tees of the House of Commons.   His clients pay not
so much for legal as for manly accomplishments, —
for courage, conduct, and a commanding social position, which enable him to make their claims heard
and respected.

I know very well that among our cool and cal-
culating people, where every man mounts guard
over himself, where heats and panics and abandon-
ments are quite out of the system, there is a good
deal of skepticism as to extraordinary influence.
To talk of an overpowering mind rouses the same
jealousy and defiance which one may observe round
a table where anybody is recounting the marvellous

anecdotes of mesmerism. Each auditor puts a final
stroke to the discourse by exclaiming, "Can he
mesmerize *me*?" So each man inquires if any
orator can change *his* convictions.

But does any one suppose himself to be quite
impregnable? Does he think that not possibly a
man may come to him who shall persuade him out
of his most settled determination? — for example,
good sedate citizen as he is, to make a fanatic of
him, — or, if he is penurious, to squander money for
some purpose he now least thinks of, — or, if he is
a prudent, industrious person, to forsake his work,
and give days and weeks to a new interest? No,
he defies any one, every one. Ah! he is thinking
of resistance, and of a different turn from his own.
But what if one should come of the same turn of
mind as his own, and who sees much farther on his
own way than he? A man who has tastes like
mine, but in greater power, will rule me any day,
and make me love my ruler.

Thus it is not powers of speech that we primarily
consider under this word *eloquence*, but the power
that being present, gives them their perfection,
and being absent, leaves them a merely superficial
value. Eloquence is the appropriate organ of the
highest personal energy. Personal ascendency may
exist with or without adequate talent for its expression. It is as surely felt as a mountain or a planet;

but when it is weaponed with a power of speech, it seems first to become truly human, works actively in all directions, and supplies the imagination with fine materials.

This circumstance enters into every consideration of the power of orators, and is the key to all their effects. In the assembly, you shall find the orator and the audience in perpetual balance; and the predominance of either is indicated by the choice of topic. If the talents for speaking exist, but not the strong personality, then there are good speakers who perfectly receive and express the will of the audience, and the commonest populace is flattered by hearing its low mind returned to it with every ornament which happy talent can add. But if there be personality in the orator, the face of things changes. The audience is thrown into the attitude of pupil, follows like a child its preceptor, and hears what he has to say. It is as if, amidst the king's council at Madrid, Ximenes urged that an advantage might be gained of France, and Mendoza that Flanders might be kept down, and Columbus, being introduced, was interrogated whether his geographical knowledge could aid the cabinet; and he can say nothing to one party or to the other, but he can show how all Europe can be diminished and reduced under the king, by annexing to Spain a continent as large as six or seven Europes.

This balance between the orator and the audience is expressed in what is called the pertinence of the speaker. There is always a rivalry between the orator and the occasion, between the demands of the hour and the prepossession of the individual. The emergency which has convened the meeting is usually of more importance than anything the debaters have in their minds, and therefore becomes imperative to them. But if one of them have anything of commanding necessity in his heart, how speedily he will find vent for it, and with the applause of the assembly! This balance is observed in the privatest intercourse. Poor Tom never knew the time when the present occurrence was so trivial that he could tell what was passing in his mind without being checked for unseasonable speech; but let Bacon speak and wise men would rather listen though the revolution of kingdoms was on foot. I have heard it reported of an eloquent preacher, whose voice is not yet forgotten in this city, that, on occasions of death or tragic disaster which overspread the congregation with gloom, he ascended the pulpit with more than his usual alacrity, and turning to his favorite lessons of devout and jubilant thankfulness, — " Let us praise the Lord," — carried audience, mourners, and mourning along with him, and swept away all the impertinence of private sorrow with his hosannas and songs of

praise. Pepys says of Lord Clarendon (with whom
" he is mad in love") on his return from a conference, " I did never observe how much easier a
man do speak when he knows all the company to
be below him, than in him; for, though he spoke
indeed excellent well, yet his manner and freedom
of doing it, as if he played with it, and was inform-
ing only all the rest of the company, was mighty
pretty." [1]

This rivalry between the orator and the occasion
is inevitable, and the occasion always yields to the
eminence of the speaker; for a great man is the
greatest of occasions. Of course the interest of the
audience and of the orator conspire. It is well
with them only when his influence is complete;
then only they are well pleased. Especially he
consults his power by making instead of taking his
theme. If he should attempt to instruct the people
in that which they already know, he would fail;
but by making them wise in that which he knows,
he has the advantage of the assembly every moment. Napoleon's tactics of marching on the angle
of an army, and always presenting a superiority of
numbers, is the orator's secret also.

The several talents which the orator employs, the
splendid weapons which went to the equipment of
Demosthenes, of Æschines, of Demades the natural

[1] Diary, I. 169.

orator, of Fox, of Pitt, of Patrick Henry, of Adams,
of Mirabeau, deserve a special enumeration. We
must not quite omit to name the principal pieces.

The orator, as we have seen, must be a substantial personality. Then, first, he must have power
of statement, — must have the fact, and know how
to tell it. In any knot of men conversing on any
subject, the person who knows most about it will
have the ear of the company if he wishes it, and
lead the conversation, no matter what genius or
distinction other men there present may have ; and
in any public assembly, him who has the facts and
can and will state them, people will listen to, though
he is otherwise ignorant, though he is hoarse and
ungraceful, though he stutters and screams.

In a court of justice the audience are impartial ;
they really wish to sift the statements and know
what the truth is. And in the examination of witnesses there usually leap out, quite unexpectedly,
three or four stubborn words or phrases which are
the pith and fate of the business, which sink into
the ear of all parties, and stick there, and determine
the cause. All the rest is repetition and qualify-
ing; and the court and the county have really come
together to arrive at these three or four memorable
expressions which betrayed the mind and meaning
of somebody.

In every company the man with the fact is like

the guide you hire to lead your party up a mountain, or through a difficult country.   He may not
compare with any of the party in mind, or breed-
ing, or courage, or possessions, but he is much
more important to the present need than any of
them.   That is what we go to the court-house for,
— the statement of the fact, and of a general fact,
the real relation of all the parties ; and it is the
certainty with which, indifferently in any affair
that is well handled, the truth stares us in the face
through all the disguises that are put upon it, — a
piece of the well-known human life, — that makes
the interest of a court-room to the intelligent spectator.

I remember long ago being attracted, by the distinction of the counsel and the local importance
of the cause, into the court-room.   The prisoner's
counsel were the strongest and cunningest lawyers
in the Commonwealth.   They drove the attorney
for the State from corner to corner, taking his rea-
sons from under him, and reducing him to silence,
but not to submission.   When hard pressed, he re-
venged himself, in his turn, on the judge, by requiring the court to define what *salvage* was.   The
court, thus pushed, tried words, and said every
thing it could think of to fill the time, supposing
cases, and describing duties of insurers, captains,
pilots, and miscellaneous sea-officers that are or

might be, — like a schoolmaster puzzled by a hard
sum, who reads the context with emphasis. But
all this flood not serving the cuttle-fish to get away
in, the horrible shark of the district-attorney being
still there, grimly awaiting with his " The court
must define," — the poor court pleaded its inferi-
ority. The superior court must establish the law
for this, and it read away piteously the decisions
of the Supreme Court, but read to those who had
no pity. The judge was forced at last to rule something, and the lawyers saved their rogue under the
fog of a definition. The parts were so well cast
and discriminated that it was an interesting game
to watch. The government was well enough rep-
resented. It was stupid, but it had a strong will
and possession, and stood on that to the last. The
judge had a task beyond his preparation, yet his
position remained real: he was there to represent a
great reality, — the justice of states, which we could
well enough see beetling over his head, and which
his trifling talk nowise affected, and did not im-
pede, since he was entirely well-meaning.

The statement of the fact, however, sinks before
the statement of the law, which requires immeasurably higher powers, and is a rarest gift, being in
all great masters one and the same thing, — in
lawyers nothing technical, but always some piece
of common-sense, alike interesting to laymen as

to clerks.   Lord Mansfield's merit is the merit of
common-sense.   It is the same quality we admire
in Aristotle, Montaigne, Cervantes, or in Samuel
Johnson, or Franklin.   Its application to law
seems quite accidental.   Each of Mansfield's famous decisions contains a level sentence or two
which hit the mark.   His sentences are not always
finished to the eye, but are finished to the mind.
The sentences are involved, but a solid proposition
is set forth, a true distinction is drawn.   They come
from and they go to the sound human understanding; and I read without surprise that the black-
letter lawyers of the day sneered at his " equitable
decisions," as if they were not also learned.   This,
indeed, is what speech is for, — to make the statement; and all that is called eloquence seems to me
of little use for the most part to those who have it,
but inestimable to such as have something to say.

Next to the knowledge of the fact and its law is
method, which constitutes the genius and efficiency
of all remarkable men.   A crowd of men go up to
Faneuil Hall; they are all pretty well acquainted
with the object of the meeting; they have all read
the facts in the same newspapers.   The orator possesses no information which his hearers have not,
yet he teaches them to see the thing with his eyes.
By the new placing, the circumstances acquire new
solidity and worth.   Every fact gains consequence

by his naming it, and trifles become important. His expressions fix themselves in men's memories, and fly from mouth to mouth. His mind has some new principle of order. Where he looks, all things fly into their places. What will he say next? Let this man speak, and this man only. By applying the habits of a higher style of thought to the common affairs of this world, he introduces beauty and magnificence wherever he goes. Such a power was Burke's, and of this genius we have had some brilliant examples in our own political and legal men.

Imagery. The orator must be, to a certain extent, a poet. We are such imaginative creatures that nothing so works on the human mind, barbarous or civil, as a trope. Condense some daily experience into a glowing symbol, and an audience is electrified. They feel as if they already possessed some new right and power over a fact which they can detach, and so completely master in thought. It is a wonderful aid to the memory, which carries away the image and never loses it. A popular assembly, like the House of Commons, or the French Chamber, or the American Congress, is commanded by these two powers, — first by a fact, then by skill of statement. Put the argument into a concrete shape, into an image, — some hard phrase, round and solid as a ball, which they can see and handle and carry home with them, — and the cause is half won.

Statement, method, imagery, selection, tenacity
of memory, power of dealing with facts, of illumi-
nating them, of sinking them by ridicule or by
diversion of the mind, rapid generalization, humor,
pathos, are keys which the orator holds; and yet
these fine gifts are not eloquence, and do often hinder a man's attainment of it.   And if we come to
the heart of the mystery, perhaps we should say
that the truly eloquent man is a sane man with
power to communicate his sanity.   If you arm the
man with the extraordinary weapons of this art,
give him a grasp of facts, learning, quick fancy, sarcasm, splendid allusion, interminable illustration,—
all these talents, so potent and charming, have an
equal power to insnare and mislead the audience
and the orator.   His talents are too much for him,
his horses run away with him; and people always
perceive whether you drive or whether the horses
take the bits in their teeth and run.   But these talents are quite something else when they are subordinated and serve him; and we go to Washington,
or to Westminster Hall, or might well go round
the world, to see a man who drives, and is not run
away with, — a man who, in prosecuting great designs, has an absolute command of the means of
representing his ideas, and uses them only to express these; placing facts, placing men; amid the
inconceivable levity of human beings, never for

an instant warped from his erectness. There is
for every man a statement possible of that truth
which he is most unwilling to receive, — a statement possible, so broad and so pungent that he
cannot get away from it, but must either bend to
it or die of it. Else there would be no such word
as eloquence, which means this. The listener cannot hide from himself that something has been
shown him and the whole world which he did not
wish to see ; and as he cannot dispose of it, it disposes of him. The history of public men and affairs in America will readily furnish tragic examples of this fatal force.

For the triumphs of the art somewhat more must
still be required, namely a reinforcing of man from
events, so as to give the double force of reason and
destiny. In transcendent eloquence, there was ever
some crisis in affairs, such as could deeply engage
the man to the cause he pleads, and draw all this
wide power to a point. For the explosions and
eruptions, there must be accumulations of heat
somewhere, beds of ignited anthracite at the centre.
And in cases where profound conviction has been
wrought, the eloquent man is he who is no beautiful speaker, but who is inwardly drunk with a certain belief. It agitates and tears him, and perhaps
almost bereaves him of the power of articulation.
Then it rushes from him as in short, abrupt screams,

in torrents of meaning. The possession the subject
has of his mind is so entire that it insures an order
of expression which is the order of Nature itself,
and so the order of greatest force, and inimitable
by any art.   And the main distinction between
him and other well-graced actors is the conviction,
communicated by every word, that his mind is con-
templating a whole, and inflamed by the contemplation of the whole, and that the words and sentences uttered by him, however admirable, fall from
him as unregarded parts of that terrible whole
which he sees and which he means that you shall
see.   Add to this concentration a certain regnant
calmness, which, in all the tumult, never utters
a premature syllable, but keeps the secret of its
means and method; and the orator stands before
the people as a demoniacal power to whose miracles
they have no key.   This terrible earnestness makes
good the ancient superstition of the hunter, that
the bullet will hit its mark, which is first dipped in
the marksman's blood.

Eloquence must be grounded on the plainest
narrative.   Afterwards, it may warm itself until it
exhales symbols of every kind and color, speaks
only through the most poetic forms ; but, first and
last, it must still be at bottom a biblical statement
of fact.   The orator is thereby an orator, that he
keeps his feet ever on a fact.   Thus only is he in-

vincible. No gifts, no graces, no power of wit or
learning or illustration will make any amends for
want of this. All audiences are just to this point.
Fame of voice or of rhetoric will carry people a
few times to hear a speaker; but they soon begin
to ask, " What is he driving at ? " and if this man
does not stand for anything, he will be deserted.
A good upholder of anything which they believe, a
fact-speaker of any kind, they will long follow;
but a pause in the speaker's own character is very
properly a loss of attraction. The preacher enu-
merates his classes of men and I do not find my
place therein; I suspect then that no man does.
Everything is my cousin; and whilst he speaks
things, I feel that he is touching some of my relations, and I am uneasy; but whilst he deals in
words we are released from attention. If you
would lift me you must be on higher ground. If
you would liberate me you must be free. If you
would correct my false view of facts, — hold up to
me the same facts in the true order of thought, and
I cannot go back from the new conviction.

The power of Chatham, of Pericles, of Luther,
rested on this strength of character, which, because
it did not and could not fear anybody, made nothing of their antagonists, and became sometimes
exquisitely provoking and sometimes terrific to
these.

We are slenderly furnished with anecdotes of these men, nor can we help ourselves by those heavy books in which their discourses are reported. Some of them were writers, like Burke; but most of them were not, and no record at all adequate to their fame remains. Besides, what is best is lost, — the fiery life of the moment. But the conditions for eloquence always exist. It is always dying out of famous places and appearing in corners. Wherever the polarities meet, wherever the fresh moral sentiment, the instinct of freedom and duty, come in direct opposition to fossil conservatism and the thirst of gain, the spark will pass. The resistance to slavery in this country has been a fruitful nursery of orators. The natural connection by which it drew to itself a train of moral reforms, and the slight yet sufficient party organization it offered, reinforced the city with new blood from the woods and mountains. Wild men, John Baptists, Hermit Peters, John Knoxes, utter the savage sentiment of Nature in the heart of commercial capitals. They send us every year some piece of aboriginal strength, some tough oak-stick of a man who is not to be silenced or insulted or intimidated by a mob, because he is more mob than they, — one who mobs the mob, — some sturdy countryman, on whom neither money, nor politeness, nor hard words, nor eggs, nor blows, nor brickbats,

make any impression. He is fit to meet the bar-
room wits and bullies; he is a wit and a bully himself, and something more: he is a graduate of the
plough, and the stub-hoe, and the bushwhacker;
knows all the secrets of swamp and snow-bank, and
has nothing to learn of labor or poverty or the
rough of farming. His hard head went through,
in childhood, the drill of Calvinism, with text and
mortification, so that he stands in the New England assembly a purer bit of New England than
any, and flings his sarcasms right and left. He
has not only the documents in his pocket to answer
all cavils and to prove all his positions, but he has
the eternal reason in his head. This man scorn-
fully renounces your civil organizations, — county,
or city, or governor, or army; — is his own navy
and artillery, judge and jury, legislature and executive. He has learned his lessons in a bitter
school. Yet, if the pupil be of a texture to bear
it, the best university that can be recommended to
a man of ideas is the gauntlet of the mobs.

He who will train himself to mastery in this
science of persuasion must lay the emphasis of education, not on popular arts, but on character and
insight. Let him see that his speech is not differ-
enced from action; that when he has spoken he has
not done nothing, nor done wrong, but has cleared
his own skirts, has engaged himself to wholesome

exertion. Let him look on opposition as opportunity. He cannot be defeated or put down. There
is a principle of resurrection in him, an immortality
of purpose. Men are averse and hostile, to give
value to their suffrages. It is not the people that
are in fault for not being convinced, but he that
cannot convince them. He should mould them,
armed as he is with the reason and love which are
also the core of their nature. He is not to neutralize their opposition, but he is to convert them into
fiery apostles and publishers of the same wisdom.

The highest platform of eloquence is the moral
sentiment. It is what is called affirmative truth,
and has the property of invigorating the hearer;
and it conveys a hint of our eternity, when he
feels himself addressed on grounds which will remain when everything else is taken, and which have
no trace of time or place or party. Everything
hostile is stricken down in the presence of the sentiments; their majesty is felt by the most obdurate.
It is observable that as soon as one acts for large
masses, the moral element will and must be allowed
for, will and must work; and the men least accustomed to appeal to these sentiments invariably recall them when they address nations. Napoleon,
even, must accept and use it as he can.

It is only to these simple strokes that the highest
power belongs, — when a weak human hand touches,

point by point, the eternal beams and rafters on
which the whole structure of Nature and society is
laid. In this tossing sea of delusion we feel with
our feet the adamant; in this dominion of chance
we find a principle of permanence. For I do not
accept that definition of Isocrates, that the office of
his art is to make the great small and the small
great; but I esteem this to be its perfection, —
when the orator sees through all masks to the eternal scale of truth, in such sort that he can hold up
before the eyes of men the fact of to-day steadily
to that standard, thereby making the great great,
and the small small, which is the true way to aston-
ish and to reform mankind.

All the chief orators of the world have been
grave men, relying on this reality. One thought
the philosophers of Demosthenes's own time found
running through all his orations, — this namely,
that " virtue secures its own success." " To stand
on one's own feet " Heeren finds the key-note to
the discourses of Demosthenes, as of Chatham.

Eloquence, like every other art, rests on laws the
most exact and determinate. It is the best speech
of the best soul. It may well stand as the exponent
of all that is grand and immortal in the mind. If
it do not so become an instrument, but aspires to be
somewhat of itself, and to glitter for show, it is
false and weak. In its right exercise, it is an elas-

tic, unexhausted power, — who has sounded, who
has estimated it? — expanding with the expansion
of our interests and affections. Its great masters,
whilst they valued every help to its attainment, and
thought no pains too great which contributed in
any manner to further it, — resembling the Arabian
warrior of fame, who wore seventeen weapons in
his belt, and in personal combat used them all occasionally, — yet subordinated all means; never
permitted any talent — neither voice, rhythm, poetic power, anecdote, sarcasm — to appear for show;
but were grave men, who preferred their integrity
to their talent, and esteemed that object for which
they toiled, whether the prosperity of their country,
or the laws, or a reformation, or liberty of speech
or of the press, or letters, or morals, as above the
whole world, and themselves also.

DOMESTIC LIFE.

DOMESTIC LIFE.

THE perfection of the providence for childhood is easily acknowledged. The care which covers the seed of the tree under tough husks and stony cases provides for the human plant the mother's breast and the father's house. The size of the nestler is comic, and its tiny beseeching weakness is compensated perfectly by the happy patronizing look of the mother, who is a sort of high reposing Providence toward it. Welcome to the parents the puny struggler, strong in his weakness, his little arms more irresistible than the soldier's, his lips touched with persuasion which Chatham and Pericles in manhood had not. His unaffected lamentations when he lifts up his voice on high, or, more beautiful, the sobbing child, — the face all liquid grief, as he tries to swallow his vexation, — soften all hearts to pity, and to mirthful and clamorous compassion. The small despot asks so little that all reason and all nature are on his side. His ignorance is more charming than all knowledge, and his little sins more bewitching than any virtue. His

flesh is angels' flesh, all alive. "Infancy," said
Coleridge, " presents body and spirit in unity: the
body is all animated." All day, between his three
or four sleeps, he coos like a pigeon-house, sputters
and spurs and puts on his faces of importance;
and when he fasts, the little Pharisee fails not to
sound his trumpet before him. By lamplight he
delights in shadows on the wall; by daylight, in
yellow and scarlet. Carry him out of doors, — he is
overpowered by the light and by the extent of natural objects, and is silent. Then presently begins
his use of his fingers, and he studies power, the lesson of his race. First it appears in no great harm,
in architectural tastes. Out of blocks, thread-
spools, cards, and checkers, he will build his pyramid with the gravity of Palladio. With an acous-
tic apparatus of whistle and rattle he explores the
laws of sound. But chiefly, like his senior country-
men, the young American studies new and speedier
modes of transportation. Mistrusting the cunning
of his small legs, he wishes to ride on the necks
and shoulders of all flesh. The small enchanter
nothing can withstand, — no seniority of age, no
gravity of character; uncles, aunts, grandsires,
grandams, fall an easy prey: he conforms to nobody, all conform to him; all caper and make
mouths and babble and chirrup to him. On the
strongest shoulders he rides, and pulls the hair of
laurelled heads.

" The childhood," said Milton, " shows the man, as morning shows the day." The child realizes to every man his own earliest remembrance, and so supplies a defect in our education, or enables us to live over the unconscious history with a sympathy so tender as to be almost personal experience.

Fast — almost too fast for the wistful curiosity of the parents, studious of the witchcraft of curls and dimples and broken words — the little talker grows to a boy. He walks daily among wonders : fire, light, darkness, the moon, the stars, the furniture of the house, the red tin horse, the domestics, who like rude foster-mothers befriend and feed him, the faces that claim his kisses, are all in turn absorbing; yet warm, cheerful, and with good appetite the little sovereign subdues them without knowing it ; the new knowledge is taken up into the life of to-day and becomes the means of more. The blowing rose is a new event ; the garden full of flowers is Eden over again to the small Adam ; the rain, the ice, the frost, make epochs in his life. What a holiday is the first snow in which Twoshoes can be trusted abroad !

What art can paint or gild any object in after-life with the glow which Nature gives to the first baubles of childhood ! St. Peter's can not have the magical power over us that the red and gold covers of our first picture-book possessed. How the imagination cleaves to the warm glories of that tinsel even now! What entertainments make every day bright and short for the fine freshman! The street is old as Nature; the persons all have their sacredness. His imaginative life dresses all things in their best. His fears adorn the dark parts with poetry. He has heard of wild horses and of bad boys, and with a pleasing terror he watches at his gate for the passing of those varieties of each species. The first ride into the country, the first bath in running water, the first time the skates are put on, the first game out of doors in moonlight, the books of the nursery, are new chapters of joy. The "Arabian Nights' Entertainments," the "Seven Champions of Christendom," "Robinson Crusoe," and the "Pilgrim's Progress," — what mines of thought and emotion, what a wardrobe to dress the whole world withal, are in this encyclopædia of young thinking! And so by beautiful traits, which without art yet seem the masterpiece of wisdom, provoking the love that watches and educates him, the little pilgrim prosecutes the journey through nature which he has thus gaily begun. He grows up the ornament and joy of the house, which rings to his glee, to rosy boyhood.

The household is the home of the man, as well as of the child. The events that occur therein are more near and affecting to us than those which

are sought in senates and academies. Domestic
events are certainly our affair. What are called
public events may or may not be ours. If a man
wishes to acquaint himself with the real history of
the world, with the spirit of the age, he must not
go first to the state-house or the court-room. The
subtle spirit of life must be sought in facts nearer.
It is what is done and suffered in the house, in the
constitution, in the temperament, in the personal
history, that has the profoundest interest for us.
Fact is better than fiction, if only we could get pure
fact. Do you think any rhetoric or any romance
would get your ear from the wise gypsy who could
tell straight on the real fortunes of the man ; who
could reconcile your moral character and your natural history ; who could explain your misfortunes,
your fevers, your debts, your temperament, your
habits of thought, your tastes, and, in every explanation, not sever you from the whole, but unite you
to it ? Is it not plain that not in senates, or courts,
or chambers of commerce, but in the dwelling-house
must the true character and hope of the time be
consulted ? These facts are, to be sure, harder to
read. It is easier to count the census, or compute
the square extent of a territory, to criticise its pol-
ity, books, art, than to come to the persons and
dwellings of men and read their character and
hope in their way of life. Yet we are always hov-

ering round this better divination. In one form or
another we are always returning to it. The physi-
ognomy and phrenology of to-day are rash and mechanical systems enough, but they rest on everlasting foundations. We are sure that the sacred form
of man is not seen in these whimsical, pitiful, and
sinister masks (masks which we wear and which
we meet), these bloated and shrivelled bodies, bald
heads, bead eyes, short winds, puny and precarious
healths, and early deaths. We live ruins amidst
ruins. The great facts are the near ones. The
account of the body is to be sought in the mind.
The history of your fortunes is written first in your
life.

Let us come then out of the public square and
enter the domestic precinct. Let us go to the sitting-room, the table-talk and the expenditure of our
contemporaries. An increased consciousness of the
soul, you say, characterizes the period. Let us see
if it has not only arranged the atoms at the circum-
ference, but the atoms at the core. Does the household obey an idea? Do you see the man, — his
form, genius, and aspiration, — in his economy? Is
that translucent, thorough-lighted? There should
be nothing confounding and conventional in economy, but the genius and love of the man so conspicuously marked in all his estate that the eye that
knew him should read his character in his property,

in his grounds, in his ornaments, in every expense. A man's money should not follow the direction of his neighbor's money, but should represent to him the things he would willingliest do with it. I am not one thing and my expenditure another. My expenditure is me. That our expenditure and our character are twain, is the vice of society.

We ask the price of many things in shops and stalls, but some things each man buys without hesitation; if it were only letters at the post-office, conveyance in carriages and boats, tools for his work, books that are written to his condition, etc. Let him never buy anything else than what he wants, never subscribe at others' instance, never give unwillingly. Thus, a scholar is a literary foundation. All his expense is for Aristotle, Fabricius, Erasmus, and Petrarch. Do not ask him to help with his savings young drapers or grocers to stock their shops, or eager agents to lobby in legislatures, or join a company to build a factory or a fishing-craft. These things are also to be done, but not by such as he. How could such a book as Plato's Dialogues have come down, but for the sacred savings of scholars and their fantastic appropriation of them?

Another man is a mechanical genius, an inventor of looms, a builder of ships, — a ship-building foundation, and could achieve nothing if he should dissi-

pate himself on books or on horses. Another is a
farmer, an agricultural foundation; another is a
chemist, and the same rule holds for all. We
must not make believe with our money, but spend
heartily, and buy *up* and not *down*.

I am afraid that, so considered, our houses will
not be found to have unity and to express the best
thought. The household, the calling, the friendships, of the citizen are not homogeneous. His
house ought to show us his honest opinion of what
makes his well-being when he rests among his kindred, and forgets all affectation, compliance, and
even exertion of will. He brings home whatever
commodities and ornaments have for years allured
his pursuit, and his character must be seen in them.
But what idea predominates in our houses? Thrift
first, then convenience and pleasure. Take off all
the roofs, from street to street, and we shall seldom
find the temple of any higher god than Prudence.
The progress of domestic living has been in clean-
liness, in ventilation, in health, in decorum, in
countless means and arts of comfort, in the concentration of all the utilities of every clime in each
house. They are arranged for low benefits. The
houses of the rich are confectioners' shops, where we
get sweetmeats and wine; the houses of the poor
are imitations of these to the extent of their ability.
With these ends housekeeping is not beautiful; it

cheers and raises neither the husband, the wife, nor
the child; neither the host nor the guest; it op-
presses women. A house kept to the end of prudence is laborious without joy ; a house kept to the
end of display is impossible to all but a few women,
and their success is dearly bought.

If we look at this matter curiously, it becomes
dangerous. We need all the force of an idea to lift
this load, for the wealth and multiplication of conveniences embarrass us, especially in northern climates. The shortest enumeration of our wants in
this rugged climate appalls us by the multitude of
things not easy to be done. And if you look at
the multitude of particulars, one would say : Good
housekeeping is impossible; order is too precious a
thing to dwell with men and women. See, in families where there is both substance and taste, at what
expense any favorite punctuality is maintained. If
the children, for example, are considered, dressed,
dieted, attended, kept in proper company, schooled,
and at home fostered by the parents, — then does
the hospitality of the house suffer; friends are less
carefully bestowed, the daily table less catered. If
the hours of meals are punctual, the apartments are
slovenly. If the linens and hangings are clean and
fine and the furniture good, the yard, the garden,
the fences are neglected. If all are well attended,
then must the master and mistress be studious of

particulars at the cost of their own accomplishments and growth; or persons are treated as
things.

The difficulties to be overcome must be freely
admitted; they are many and great. Nor are they
to be disposed of by any criticism or amendment of
particulars taken one at a time, but only by the
arrangement of the household to a higher end than
those to which our dwellings are usually built and
furnished. And is there any calamity more grave,
or that more invokes the best good-will to remove
it, than this? — to go from chamber to chamber
and see no beauty; to find in the housemates no
aim; to hear an endless chatter and blast; to be
compelled to criticise; to hear only to dissent and to
be disgusted; to find no invitation to what is good
in us, and no receptacle for what is wise: — this
is a great price to pay for sweet bread and warm
lodging, — being defrauded of affinity, of repose,
of genial culture, and the inmost presence of
beauty.

It is a sufficient accusation of our ways of living,
and certainly ought to open our ear to every good-
minded reformer, that our idea of domestic well-
being now needs wealth to execute it. Give me the
means, says the wife, and your house shall not annoy your taste nor waste your time. On hearing
this we understand how these Means have come to

be so omnipotent on earth. And indeed the love of
wealth seems to grow chiefly out of the root of the
love of the Beautiful. The desire of gold is not for
gold. It is not the love of much wheat and wool
and household-stuff. It is the means of freedom
and benefit. We scorn shifts; we desire the ele-
gance of munificence; we desire at least to put no
stint or limit on our parents, relatives, guests or dependents; we desire to play the benefactor and the
prince with our townsmen, with the stranger at the
gate, with the bard or the beauty, with the man or
woman of worth who alights at our door. How
can we do this, if the wants of each day imprison
us in lucrative labors, and constrain us to a contin-
ual vigilance lest we be betrayed into expense?

Give us wealth, and the home shall exist. But
that is a very imperfect and inglorious solution of
the problem, and therefore no solution. "*Give us
wealth.*" You ask too much. Few have wealth,
but all must have a home. Men are not born rich;
and in getting wealth the man is generally sacrificed, and often is sacrificed without acquiring
wealth at last. Besides, that cannot be the right
answer;—there are objections to wealth. Wealth
is a shift. The wise man angles with himself only,
and with no meaner bait. Our whole use of wealth
needs revision and reform. Generosity does not
consist in giving money or money's worth. These

so-called *goods* are only the shadow of good. To give money to a sufferer is only a come-off. It is only a postponement of the real payment, a bribe paid for silence, a credit-system in which a paper promise to pay answers for the time instead of liquidation. We owe to man higher succors than food and fire. We owe to man man. If he is sick, is unable, is mean-spirited and odious, it is because there is so much of his nature which is unlawfully withholden from him. He should be visited in this his prison with rebuke to the evil demons, with manly encouragement, with no mean-spirited offer of condolence because you have not money, or mean offer of money as the utmost benefit, but by your heroism, your purity, and your faith. You are to bring with you that spirit which is understanding, health and self-help. To offer him money in lieu of these is to do him the same wrong as when the bridegroom offers his betrothed virgin a sum of money to release him from his engagements. The great depend on their heart, not on their purse. Genius and virtue, like diamonds, are best plain-set, — set in lead, set in poverty. The greatest man in history was the poorest. How was it with the captains and sages of Greece and Rome, with Socrates, with Epaminondas? Aristides was made general receiver of Greece, to collect the tribute which each state was to furnish against the barba-

rian. " Poor," says Plutarch, " when he set about
it, poorer when he had finished it." How was it
with Æmilius and Cato? What kind of a house
was kept by Paul and John, by Milton and Marvell, by Samuel Johnson, by Samuel Adams in
Boston, and Jean Paul Richter at Baireuth?

I think it plain that this voice of communities
and ages, ' Give us wealth, and the good household
shall exist,' is vicious, and leaves the whole difficulty untouched. It is better, certainly, in this
form, ' Give us your labor, and the household begins.' I see not how serious labor, the labor of all
and every day, is to be avoided ; and many things
betoken a revolution of opinion and practice in
regard to manual labor that may go far to aid our
practical inquiry. Another age may divide the
manual labor of the world more equally on all the
members of society, and so make the labors of a
few hours avail to the wants and add to the vigor
of the man. But the reform that applies itself to
the household must not be partial. It must correct
the whole system of our social living. It must come
with plain living and high thinking ; it must break
up caste, and put domestic service on another foundation. It must come in connection with a true
acceptance by each man of his vocation, — not
chosen by his parents or friends, but by his genius,
with earnestness and love.

Nor is this redress so hopeless as it seems. Certainly, if we begin by reforming particulars of our present system, correcting a few evils and letting the rest stand, we shall soon give up in despair. For our social forms are very far from truth and equity. But the way to set the axe at the root of the tree is to raise our aim. Let us understand then that a house should bear witness in all its economy that human culture is the end to which it is built and garnished. It stands there under the sun and moon to ends analogous, and not less noble than theirs. It is not for festivity, it is not for sleep: but the pine and the oak shall gladly descend from the mountains to uphold the roof of men as faithful and necessary as themselves; to be the shelter always open to good and true persons; — a hall which shines with sincerity, brows ever tranquil, and a demeanor impossible to disconcert; whose inmates know what they want; who do not ask your house how theirs should be kept. They have aims; they cannot pause for trifles. The diet of the house does not create its order, but knowledge, character, action, absorb so much life and yield so much entertainment that the refectory has ceased to be so curiously studied. With a change of aim has followed a change of the whole scale by which men and things were wont to be measured. Wealth and poverty are seen for what they are.

It begins to be seen that the poor are only they who feel poor, and poverty consists in feeling poor. The rich, as we reckon them, and among them the very rich, — in a true scale would be found very indigent and ragged. The great make us feel, first of all, the indifference of circumstances. They call into activity the higher perceptions and subdue the low habits of comfort and luxury; but the higher perceptions find their objects everywhere; only the low habits need palaces and banquets.

Let a man, then, say, My house is here in the county, for the culture of the county; — an eating-house and sleeping-house for travellers it shall be, but it shall be much more. I pray you, O excellent wife, not to cumber yourself and me to get a rich dinner for this man or this woman who has alighted at our gate, nor a bedchamber made ready at too great a cost. These things, if they are curious in them, they can get for a dollar at any village. But let this stranger, if he will, in your looks, in your accent and behavior, read your heart and earnestness, your thought and will, which he cannot buy at any price, in any village or city; and which he may well travel fifty miles, and dine sparely and sleep hard in order to behold. Certainly, let the board be spread and let the bed be dressed for the traveller; but let not the emphasis of hospitality lie in these things. Honor to the

house where they are simple to the verge of hard-
ship, so that there the intellect is awake and reads
the laws of the universe, the soul worships truth
and love, honor and courtesy flow into all deeds.

There was never a country in the world which
could so easily exhibit this heroism as ours ; never
any where the State has made such efficient provis-
ion for popular education, where intellectual entertainment is so within reach of youthful ambition.
The poor man's son is educated.   There is many a
humble house in every city, in every town, where
talent and taste and sometimes genius dwell with
poverty and labor.   Who has not seen, and who can
see unmoved, under a low roof, the eager, blushing
boys discharging as they can their household chores,
and hastening into the sitting-room to the study of
to-morrow's merciless lesson, yet stealing time to
read one chapter more of the novel hardly smuggled
into the tolerance of father and mother, — atoning
for the same by some pages of Plutarch or Goldsmith ; the warm sympathy with which they kindle
each other in school-yard or in barn or wood-shed
with scraps of poetry or song, with phrases of the
last oration, or mimicry of the orator ; the youthful
criticism, on Sunday, of the sermons ; the school
declamation faithfully rehearsed at home, sometimes to the fatigue, sometimes to the admiration
of sisters ; the first solitary joys of literary vanity,

when the translation or the theme has been completed, sitting alone near the top of the house : the cautious comparison of the attractive advertisement of the arrival of Macready, Booth, or Kemble, or of the discourse of a well-known speaker, with the expense of the entertainment ; the affectionate delight with which they greet the return of each one after the early separations which school or business require ; the foresight with which, during such absences, they hive the honey which opportunity offers, for the ear and imagination of the others ; and the unrestrained glee with which they disburden themselves of their early mental treasures when the holidays bring them again together ? What is the hoop that holds them stanch ? It is the iron band of poverty, of necessity, of austerity, which, excluding them from the sensual enjoyments which make other boys too early old, has directed their activity in safe and right channels, and made them, despite themselves, reverers of the grand, the beautiful, and the good. Ah ! short-sighted students of books, of Nature, and of man ! too happy, could they know their advantages. They pine for freedom from that mild parental yoke ; they sigh for fine clothes, for rides, for the theatre, and premature freedom and dissipation, which others possess. Woe to them if their wishes were crowned ! The angels that dwell with them and are weaving lau-

rels of life for their youthful brows, are Toil and
Want, and Truth, and Mutual Faith.

In many parts of true economy a cheering lesson
may be learned from the mode of life and manners
of the later Romans, as described to us in the letters
of the younger Pliny. Nor can I resist the temptation of quoting so trite an instance as the noble
housekeeping of Lord Falkland in Clarendon: "His
house being within little more than ten miles from
Oxford, he contracted familiarity and friendship
with the most polite and accurate men of that University, who found such an immenseness of wit and
such a solidity of judgment in him, so infinite a
fancy, bound in by a most logical ratiocination, such
a vast knowledge that he was not ignorant in anything, yet such an excessive humility, as if he had
known nothing, that they frequently resorted and
dwelt with him, as in a college situated in a purer
air; so that his house was a university in a less
volume, whither they came, not so much for repose
as study, and to examine and refine those grosser
propositions which laziness and consent made current in vulgar conversation."

I honor that man whose ambition it is, not to win
laurels in the state or the army, not to be a jurist
or a naturalist, not to be a poet or a commander,
but to be a master of living well, and to administer
the offices of master or servant, of husband, father,

and friend. But it requires as much breadth of
power for this as for those other functions, — as
much, or more, — and the reason for the failure is
the same. I think the vice of our housekeeping is
that it does not hold man sacred. The vice of government, the vice of education, the vice of religion,
is one with that of private life.

In the old fables we used to read of a cloak
brought from fairy-land as a gift for the fairest and
purest in Prince Arthur's court. It was to be her
prize whom it would fit. Every one was eager to
try it on, but it would fit nobody : for one it was
a world too wide, for the next it dragged on the
ground, and for the third it shrunk to a scarf.
They, of course, said that the devil was in the mantle, for really the truth was in the mantle, and was
exposing the ugliness which each would fain conceal. All drew back with terror from the garment.
The innocent Genelas alone could wear it. In like
manner, every man is provided in his thought with
a measure of man which he applies to every passenger. Unhappily, not one in many thousands comes
up to the stature and proportions of the model.
Neither does the measurer himself; neither do the
people in the street; neither do the select individuals whom he admires, — the heroes of the race.
When he inspects them critically, he discovers that
their aims are low, that they are too quickly satis-

fied. He observes the swiftness with which life
culminates, and the humility of the expectations of
the greatest part of men. To each occurs, soon after
the age of puberty, some event or society or way
of living, which becomes the crisis of life and the
chief fact in their history. In woman, it is love and
marriage (which is more reasonable) ; and yet it is
pitiful to date and measure all the facts and sequel
of an unfolding life from such a youthful and generally inconsiderate period as the age of courtship
and marriage. In men, it is their place of education, choice of an employment, settlement in a town,
or removal to the East or to the West, or some
other magnified trifle which makes the meridian
moment, and all the after years and actions only
derive interest from their relation to that. Hence
it comes that we soon catch the trick of each man's
conversation, and knowing his two or three main
facts, anticipate what he thinks of each new topic
that rises. It is scarcely less perceivable in educated men, so called, than in the uneducated. I
have seen finely endowed men at college festivals,
ten, twenty years after they had left the halls, returning, as it seemed, the same boys who went
away. The same jokes pleased, the same straws
tickled ; the manhood and offices they brought
thither at this return seemed mere ornamental
masks ; underneath they were boys yet. We never

come to be citizens of the world, but are still villagers, who think that every thing in their petty town is a little superior to the same thing anywhere else. In each the circumstance signalized differs, but in each it is made the coals of an ever-burning egotism. In one, it was his going to sea; in a second, the difficulties he combated in going to college; in a third, his journey to the West, or his voyage to Canton; in a fourth, his coming out of the Quaker Society; in a fifth, his new diet and regimen; in a sixth, his coming forth from the abolition organizations; and in a seventh, his going into them. It is a life of toys and trinkets. We are too easily pleased.

I think this sad result appears in the manners. The men we see in each other do not give us the image and likeness of man. The men we see are whipped through the world; they are harried, wrinkled, anxious; they all seem the hacks of some invisible riders. How seldom do we behold tranquillity! We have never yet seen a man. We do not know the majestic manners that belong to him, which appease and exalt the beholder. There are no divine persons with us, and the multitude do not hasten to be divine. And yet we hold fast, all our lives long, a faith in a better life, in better men, in clean and noble relations, notwithstanding our total inexperience of a true society. Certainly this was not the intention of nature, to produce, with all this immense expenditure of means and power, so cheap and humble a result. The aspirations in the heart after the good and true teach us better, — nay, the men themselves suggest a better life.

Every individual nature has its own beauty. One is struck in every company, at every fireside, with the riches of nature, when he hears so many new tones, all musical, sees in each person original manners, which have a proper and peculiar charm, and reads new expressions of face. He perceives that nature has laid for each the foundations of a divine building, if the soul will build thereon. There is no face, no form, which one cannot in fancy associate with great power of intellect or with generosity of soul. In our experience, to be sure, beauty is not, as it ought to be, the dower of man and of woman as invariably as sensation. Beauty is, even in the beautiful, occasional, — or, as one has said, culminating and perfect only a single moment, before which it is unripe, and after which it is on the wane. But beauty is never quite absent from our eyes. Every face, every figure, suggests its own right and sound estate. Our friends are not their own highest form. But let the hearts they have agitated witness what power has lurked in the traits of these structures of clay

that pass and repass us! The secret power of form
over the imagination and affections transcends all
our philosophy. The first glance we meet may satisfy us that matter is the vehicle of higher powers
than its own, and that no laws of line or surface
can ever account for the inexhaustible expressiveness of form. We see heads that turn on the pivot
of the spine, — no more; and we see heads that
seem to turn on a pivot as deep as the axle of the
world, — so slow, and lazily, and great, they move.
We see on the lip of our companion the presence
or absence of the great masters of thought and
poetry to his mind. We read in his brow, on meeting him after many years, that he is where we left
him, or that he has made great strides.

Whilst thus nature and the hints we draw from
man suggest a true and lofty life, a household equal
to the beauty and grandeur of this world, especially
we learn the same lesson from those best relations
to individual men which the heart is always prompt-
ing us to form. Happy will that house be in which
the relations are formed from character; after the
highest, and not after the lowest order; the house
in which character marries, and not confusion and
a miscellany of unavowable motives. Then shall
marriage be a covenant to secure to either party
the sweetness and honor of being a calm, continu-
ing, inevitable benefactor to the other. Yes, and

the sufficient reply to the skeptic who doubts the competence of man to elevate and to be elevated is in that desire and power to stand in joyful and ennobling intercourse with individuals, which makes the faith and the practice of all reasonable men.

The ornament of a house is the friends who frequent it. There is no event greater in life than the appearance of new persons about our hearth, except it be the progress of the character which draws them. It has been finely added by Landor to his definition of the *great man,* "It is he who can call together the most select company when it pleases him." A verse of the old Greek Menander remains, which runs in translation : —

> " Not on the store of sprightly wine,
>   Nor plenty of delicious meats,
> Though generous Nature did design
>   To court us with perpetual treats, —
> 'T is not on these we for content depend,
> So much as on the shadow of a Friend."

It is the happiness which, where it is truly known, postpones all other satisfactions, and makes politics and commerce and churches cheap. For we figure to ourselves, — do we not? — that when men shall meet as they should, as states meet, — each a benefactor, a shower of falling stars, so rich with deeds, with thoughts, with so much accomplishment, — it shall be the festival of nature, which all

things symbolize; and perhaps Love is only the
highest symbol of Friendship, as all other things
seem symbols of love. In the progress of each
man's character, his relations to the best men, which
at first seem only the romances of youth, acquire a
graver importance; and he will have learned the
lesson of life who is skilful in the ethics of friendship.

Beyond its primary ends of the conjugal, parental, and amicable relations, the household should
cherish the beautiful arts and the sentiment of ven-
eration.

1. Whatever brings the dweller into a finer life,
what educates his eye, or ear, or hand, whatever
purifies and enlarges him, may well find place there.
And yet let him not think that a property in beautiful objects is necessary to his apprehension of them,
and seek to turn his house into a museum. Rather
let the noble practice of the Greeks find place in
our society, and let the creations of the plastic arts
be collected with care in galleries by the piety and
taste of the people, and yielded as freely as the sunlight to all. Meantime, be it remembered, we are
artists ourselves, and competitors, each one, with
Phidias and Raphael in the production of what is
graceful or grand. The fountain of beauty is the
heart, and every generous thought illustrates the

walls of your chamber. Why should we owe our power of attracting our friends to pictures and vases, to cameos and architecture? Why should we convert ourselves into showmen and appendages to our fine houses and our works of art? If by love and nobleness we take up into ourselves the beauty we admire, we shall spend it again on all around us. The man, the woman, needs not the embellishment of canvas and marble, whose every act is a subject for the sculptor, and to whose eye the gods and nymphs never appear ancient, for they know by heart the whole instinct of majesty.

I do not undervalue the fine instruction which statues and pictures give. But I think the public museum in each town will one day relieve the private house of this charge of owning and exhibiting them. I go to Rome and see on the walls of the Vatican the Transfiguration, painted by Raphael, reckoned the first picture in the world; or in the Sistine Chapel I see the grand sibyls and prophets, painted in fresco by Michel Angelo, — which have every day now for three hundred years inflamed the imagination and exalted the piety of what vast multitudes of men of all nations! I wish to bring home to my children and my friends copies of these admirable forms, which I can find in the shops of the engravers; but I do not wish the vexation of owning them. I wish to find in my own

town a library and museum which is the property
of the town, where I can deposit this precious treasure, where I and my children can see it from time
to time, and where it has its proper place among
hundreds of such donations from other citizens who
have brought thither whatever articles they have
judged to be in their nature rather a public than a
private property.

A collection of this kind, the property of each
town, would dignify the town, and we should love
and respect our neighbors more. Obviously, it
would be easy for every town to discharge this
truly municipal duty. Every one of us would
gladly contribute his share; and the more gladly,
the more considerable the institution had become.

2. Certainly, not aloof from this homage to
beauty, but in strict connection therewith, the house
will come to be esteemed a Sanctuary. The language of a ruder age has given to common law the
maxim that every man's house is his castle: the
progress of truth will make every house a shrine.
Will not man one day open his eyes and see how
dear he is to the soul of Nature, — how near it is
to him? Will he not see, through all he miscalls
accident, that Law prevails for ever and ever; that
his private being is a part of it; that its home is
in his own unsounded heart; that his economy, his

labor, his good and bad fortune, his health and
manners are all a curious and exact demonstration in
miniature of the Genius of the Eternal Providence?
When he perceives the Law, he ceases to despond.
Whilst he sees it, every thought and act is raised,
and becomes an act of religion. Does the consecration of Sunday confess the desecration of the entire
week? Does the consecration of the church confess the profanation of the house? Let us read
the incantation backward. Let the man stand on
his feet. Let religion cease to be occasional; and
the pulses of thought that go to the borders of the
universe, let them proceed from the bosom of the
Household.

These are the consolations, — these are the ends
to which the household is instituted and the rooftree
stands. If these are sought and in any good degree
attained, can the State, can commerce, can climate,
can the labor of many for one, yield anything better,
or half as good? Beside these aims, Society is
weak and the State an intrusion. I think that the
heroism which at this day would make on us the
impression of Epaminondas and Phocion must be
that of a domestic conqueror. He who shall bravely
and gracefully subdue this Gorgon of Convention
and Fashion, and show men how to lead a clean,
handsome, and heroic life amid the beggarly elements of our cities and villages; whoso shall teach

me how to eat my meat and take my repose and deal with men, without any shame following, will restore the life of man to splendor, and make his own name dear to all history.

FARMING.

FARMING.

The glory of the farmer is that, in the division of labors, it is his part to create. All trade rests at last on his primitive activity. He stands close to nature; he obtains from the earth the bread and the meat. The food which was not, he causes to be. The first farmer was the first man, and all historic nobility rests on possession and use of land. Men do not like hard work, but every man has an exceptional respect for tillage, and a feeling that this is the original calling of his race, that he himself is only excused from it by some circumstance which made him delegate it for a time to other hands. If he have not some skill which recommends him to the farmer, some product for which the farmer will give him corn, he must himself return into his due place among the planters. And the profession has in all eyes its ancient charm, as standing nearest to God, the first cause.

Then the beauty of nature, the tranquillity and innocence of the countryman, his independence, and his pleasing arts, — the care of bees, of poultry, of sheep, of cows, the dairy, the care of hay, of fruits, of orchards and forests, and the reaction of these on the workman, in giving him a strength and plain dignity like the face and manners of nature, — all men acknowledge. All men keep the farm in reserve as an asylum where, in case of mischance, to hide their poverty, — or a solitude, if they do not succeed in society. And who knows how many glances of remorse are turned this way from the bankrupts of trade, from mortified pleaders in courts and senates, or from the victims of idleness and pleasure? Poisoned by town life and town vices, the sufferer resolves: ' Well, my children, whom I have injured, shall go back to the land, to be recruited and cured by that which should have been my nursery, and now shall be their hospital.'

The farmer's office is precise and important, but you must not try to paint him in rose-color; you cannot make pretty compliments to fate and gravitation, whose minister he is. He represents the necessities. It is the beauty of the great economy of the world that makes his comeliness. He bends to the order of the seasons, the weather, the soils and crops, as the sails of a ship bend to the wind. He represents continuous hard labor, year in, year out, and small gains. He is a slow person, timed to nature, and not to city watches. He takes the pace of seasons, plants, and chemistry. Nature

never hurries : atom by atom, little by little, she
achieves her work. The lesson one learns in fishing, yachting, hunting, or planting, is the manners
of Nature ; patience with the delays of wind and
sun, delays of the seasons, bad weather, excess or
lack of water, — patience with the slowness of our
feet, with the parsimony of our strength, with the
largeness of sea and land we must traverse, etc.
The farmer times himself to Nature, and acquires
that livelong patience which belongs to her. Slow,
narrow man, his rule is that the earth shall feed
and clothe him ; and he must wait for his crop to
grow. His entertainments, his liberties and his
spending must be on a farmer's scale, and not on a
merchant's. It were as false for farmers to use a
wholesale and massy expense, as for states to use a
minute economy. But if thus pinched on one side,
he has compensatory advantages. He is permanent,
clings to his land as the rocks do. In the town
where I live, farms remain in the same families for
seven and eight generations ; and most of the
first settlers (in 1635), should they reappear on
the farms to-day, would find their own blood and
names still in possession. And the like fact holds
in the surrounding towns.

This hard work will always be done by one kind
of man ; not by scheming speculators, nor by soldiers, nor professors, nor readers of Tennyson ; but

by men of endurance — deep-chested, long-winded, tough, slow and sure, and timely. The farmer has a great health, and the appetite of health, and means to his end ; he has broad lands for his home, wood to burn great fires, plenty of plain food ; his milk at least is unwatered ; and for sleep, he has cheaper and better and more of it than citizens.

He has grave trusts confided to him. In the great household of Nature, the farmer stands at the door of the bread-room, and weighs to each his loaf. It is for him to say whether men shall marry or not. Early marriages and the number of births are indissolubly connected with abundance of food; or, as Burke said, "Man breeds at the mouth." Then he is the Board of Quarantine. The farmer is a hoarded capital of health, as the farm is the capital of wealth ; and it is from him that the health and power, moral and intellectual, of the cities came. The city is always recruited from the country. The men in cities who are the centres of energy, the driving-wheels of trade, politics, or practical arts, and the women of beauty and genius, are the children or grandchildren of farmers, and are spending the energies which their fathers' hardy, silent life accumulated in frosty furrows, in poverty, necessity, and darkness.

He is the continuous benefactor. He who digs a well, constructs a stone fountain, plants a grove

of trees by the roadside, plants an orchard, builds
a durable house, reclaims a swamp, or so much as
puts a stone seat by the wayside, makes the land
so far lovely and desirable, makes a fortune which
he cannot carry away with him, but which is useful
to his country long afterwards. The man that
works at home helps society at large with somewhat more of certainty than he who devotes himself to charities. If it be true that, not by votes
of political parties but by the eternal laws of political economy, slaves are driven out of a slave State
as fast as it is surrounded by free States, then the
true abolitionist is the farmer, who, heedless of
laws and constitutions, stands all day in the field,
investing his labor in the land, and making a product with which no forced labor can compete.

We commonly say that the rich man can speak
the truth, can afford honesty, can afford independence of opinion and action; — and that is the theory of nobility. But it is the rich man in a true
sense, that is to say, not the man of large income
and large expenditure, but solely the man whose
outlay is less than his income and is steadily kept so.

In English factories, the boy that watches the
loom, to tie the thread when the wheel stops to indicate that a thread is broken, is called a *minder*.
And in this great factory of our Copernican globe,
shifting its slides, rotating its constellations, times,

and tides, bringing now the day of planting, then of watering, then of weeding, then of reaping, then of curing and storing, — the farmer is the *minder*. His machine is of colossal proportions; the diameter of the water-wheel, the arms of the levers, the power of the battery, are out of all mechanic measure; and it takes him long to understand its parts and its working. This pump never "sucks;" these screws are never loose; this machine is never out of gear; the vat and piston, wheels and tires, never wear out, but are self-repairing.

Who are the farmer's servants? Not the Irish, nor the coolies, but Geology and Chemistry, the quarry of the air, the water of the brook, the lightning of the cloud, the castings of the worm, the plough of the frost. Long before he was born, the sun of ages decomposed the rocks, mellowed his land, soaked it with light and heat, covered it with vegetable film, then with forests, and accumulated the sphagnum whose decays made the peat of his meadow.

Science has shown the great circles in which nature works; the manner in which marine plants balance the marine animals, as the land plants supply the oxygen which the animals consume, and the animals the carbon which the plants absorb. These activities are incessant. Nature works on a method of *all for each and each for all*. The

strain that is made on one point bears on every
arch and foundation of the structure. There is a
perfect solidarity. You cannot detach an atom
from its holdings, or strip off from it the electricity, gravitation, chemic affinity, or the relation to
light and heat, and leave the atom bare. No, it
brings with it its universal ties.

Nature, like a cautious testator, ties up her estate
so as not to bestow it all on one generation, but has
a forelooking tenderness and equal regard to the
next and the next, and the fourth and the fortieth
age. There lie the inexhaustible magazines. The
eternal rocks, as we call them, have held their oxygen or lime undiminished, entire, as it was. No
particle of oxygen can rust or wear, but has the
same energy as on the first morning. The good
rocks, those patient waiters, say to him : ' We have
the sacred power as we received it. We have not
failed of our trust, and now, — when in our immense day the hour is at last struck — take the gas
we have hoarded, mingle it with water, and let it
be free to grow in plants and animals and obey the
thought of man.'

The earth works for him ; the earth is a machine
which yields almost gratuitous service to every application of intellect. Every plant is a manufac-
turer of soil. In the stomach of the plant develop-
ment begins. The tree can draw on the whole air,

the whole earth, on all the rolling main. The plant is all suction-pipe, — imbibing from the ground by its root, from the air by its leaves, with all its might.

The air works for him. The atmosphere, a sharp solvent, drinks the essence and spirit of every solid on the globe, — a menstruum which melts the mountains into it. Air is matter subdued by heat. As the sea is the grand receptacle of all rivers, so the air is the receptacle from which all things spring, and into which they all return. The invisible and creeping air takes form and solid mass. Our senses are skeptics, and believe only the impression of the moment, and do not believe the chemical fact that these huge mountain-chains are made up of gases and rolling wind. But Nature is as subtle as she is strong. She turns her capital day by day; deals never with dead, but ever with quick subjects. All things are flowing, even those that seem immovable. The adamant is always passing into smoke. The plants imbibe the materials which they want from the air and the ground. They burn, that is, exhale and decompose their own bodies into the air and earth again. The animal burns, or undergoes the like perpetual consumption. The earth burns, the mountains burn and decompose, slower, but incessantly. It is almost inevitable to push the generalization up into higher parts of nature, rank over rank into sentient beings. Nations burn with internal fire of thought and affection, which wastes while it works. We shall find finer combustion and finer fuel. Intellect is a fire : rash and pitiless it melts this wonderful bone-house which is called man. Genius even, as it is the greatest good, is the greatest harm. Whilst all thus burns, — the universe in a blaze kindled from the torch of the sun, — it needs a perpetual tempering, a phlegm, a sleep, atmospheres of azote, deluges of water, to check the fury of the conflagration ; a hoarding to check the spending, a centripetence equal to the centrifugence ; and this is invariably supplied.

The railroad dirt-cars are good excavators, but there is no porter like Gravitation, who will bring down any weights which man cannot carry, and if he wants aid, knows where to find his fellow laborers. Water works in masses, and sets its irresistible shoulder to your mills or your ships, or transports vast boulders of rock in its iceberg a thousand miles. But its far greater power depends on its talent of becoming little, and entering the smallest holes and pores. By this agency, carrying in solution elements needful to every plant, the vegetable world exists.

But as I said, we must not paint the farmer in rose-color. Whilst these grand energies have

wrought for him and made his task possible, he
is habitually engaged in small economies, and is
taught the power that lurks in petty things. Great
is the force of a few simple arrangements; for instance, the powers of a fence. On the prairie you
wander a hundred miles and hardly find a stick or
a stone. At rare intervals a thin oak-opening has
been spared, and every such section has been long
occupied. But the farmer manages to procure wood
from far, puts up a rail-fence, and at once the seeds
sprout and the oaks rise. It was only browsing
and fire which had kept them down. Plant fruit-
trees by the roadside, and their fruit will never be
allowed to ripen. Draw a pine fence about them,
and for fifty years they mature for the owner their
delicate fruit. There is a great deal of enchant-
ment in a chestnut rail or picketed pine boards.

Nature suggests every economical expedient
somewhere on a great scale. Set out a pine-tree,
and it dies in the first year, or lives a poor spindle.
But Nature drops a pine-cone in Mariposa, and it
lives fifteen centuries, grows three or four hundred
feet high, and thirty in diameter, — grows in a
grove of giants, like a colonnade of Thebes. Ask
the tree how it was done. It did not grow on a
ridge, but in a basin, where it found deep soil, cold
enough and dry enough for the pine; defended itself from the sun by growing in groves, and from

the wind by the walls of the mountain. The roots
that shot deepest, and the stems of happiest exposure, drew the nourishment from the rest, until the
less thrifty perished and manured the soil for the
stronger, and the mammoth Sequoias rose to their
enormous proportions. The traveller who saw them
remembered his orchard at home, where every year,
in the destroying wind, his forlorn trees pined like
suffering virtue. In September, when the pears
hang heaviest and are taking from the sun their
gay colors, comes usually a gusty day which shakes
the whole garden and throws down the heaviest
fruit in bruised heaps. The planter took the hint
of the Sequoias, built a high wall, or — better —
surrounded the orchard with a nursery of birches
and evergreens. Thus he had the mountain basin
in miniature ; and his pears grew to the size of
melons, and the vines beneath them ran an eighth
of a mile. But this shelter creates a new climate.
The wall that keeps off the strong wind keeps off
the cold wind. The high wall reflecting the heat
back on the soil gives that acre a quadruple share
of sunshine, —

> "Enclosing in the garden square
> A dead and standing pool of air,"

and makes a little Cuba within it, whilst all without is Labrador.

The chemist comes to his aid every year by following out some new hint drawn from nature, and now affirms that this dreary space occupied by the farmer is needless; he will concentrate his kitchen-garden into a box of one or two rods square, will take the roots into his laboratory; the vines and stalks and stems may go sprawling about in the fields outside, he will attend to the roots in his tub, gorge them with food that is good for them. The smaller his garden, the better he can feed it, and the larger the crop. As he nursed his Thanksgiving turkeys on bread and milk, so he will pamper his peaches and grapes on the viands they like best. If they have an appetite for potash, or salt, or iron, or ground bones, or even now and then for a dead hog, he will indulge them. They keep the secret well, and never tell on your table whence they drew their sunset complexion or their delicate flavors.

See what the farmer accomplishes by a cartload of tiles : he alters the climate by letting off water which kept the land cold through constant evaporation, and allows the warm rain to bring down into the roots the temperature of the air and of the surface-soil ; and he deepens the soil, since the discharge of this standing water allows the roots of his plants to penetrate below the surface to the subsoil, and accelerates the ripening of the crop. The town of Concord is one of the oldest towns in this country, far on now in its third century. The se-

lectmen have once in every five years perambulated
the boundaries, and yet, in this very year, a large
quantity of land has been discovered and added to
the town without a murmur of complaint from any
quarter. By drainage we went down to a subsoil
we did not know, and have found there is a Concord under old Concord, which we are now getting
the best crops from; a Middlesex under Middlesex; and, in fine, that Massachusetts has a base-
ment story more valuable and that promises to pay
a better rent than all the superstructure. But these
tiles have acquired by association a new interest.
These tiles are political economists, confuters of
Malthus and Ricardo; they are so many Young
Americans announcing a better era, — more bread.
They drain the land, make it sweet and friable;
have made English Chat Moss a garden, and will
now do as much for the Dismal Swamp. But beyond this benefit they are the text of better opinions and better auguries for mankind.

There has been a nightmare bred in England of
indigestion and spleen among landlords and loom-
lords, namely, the dogma that men breed too fast
for the powers of the soil; that men multiply in
a geometrical ratio, whilst corn multiplies only in
an arithmetical; and hence that, the more prosper-
ous we are, the faster we approach these frightful
limits: nay, the plight of every new generation

is worse than of the foregoing, because the first comers take up the best lands; the next, the second best; and each succeeding wave of population is driven to poorer, so that the land is ever yielding less returns to enlarging hosts of eaters. Henry Carey of Philadelphia replied: "Not so, Mr. Malthus, but just the opposite of so is the fact."

The first planter, the savage, without helpers, without tools, looking chiefly to safety from his enemy, — man or beast, — takes poor land. The better lands are loaded with timber, which he cannot clear; they need drainage, which he cannot attempt. He cannot plough, or fell trees, or drain the rich swamp. He is a poor creature; he scratches with a sharp stick, lives in a cave or a hutch, has no road but the trail of the moose or bear; he lives on their flesh when he can kill one, on roots and fruits when he cannot. He falls, and is lame; he coughs, he has a stitch in his side, he has a fever and chills; when he is hungry, he cannot always kill and eat a bear, — chances of war, — sometimes the bear eats him. 'T is long before he digs or plants at all, and then only a patch. Later he learns that his planting is better than hunting; that the earth works faster for him than he can work for himself, — works for him when he is asleep, when it rains, when heat overcomes him. The sunstroke which knocks him down brings his

corn up. As his family thrive, and other planters
come up around him, he begins to fell trees and
clear good land; and when, by and by, there is
more skill, and tools and roads, the new generations are strong enough to open the lowlands, where
the wash of mountains has accumulated the best
soil, which yield a hundred-fold the former crops.
The last lands are the best lands. It needs science
and great numbers to cultivate the best lands, and
in the best manner. Thus true political economy
is not mean, but liberal, and on the pattern of the
sun and sky. Population increases in the ratio of
morality; credit exists in the ratio of morality.

Meantime we cannot enumerate the incidents
and agents of the farm without reverting to their
influence on the farmer. He carries out this cumulative preparation of means to their last effect.
This crust of soil which ages have refined he re-
fines again for the feeding of a civil and instructed
people. The great elements with which he deals
cannot leave him unaffected, or unconscious of his
ministry; but their influence somewhat resembles
that which the same Nature has on the child, — of
subduing and silencing him. We see the farmer
with pleasure and respect when we think what powers and utilities are so meekly worn. He knows
every secret of labor; he changes the face of the
landscape. Put him on a new planet and he would

know where to begin; yet there is no arrogance in
his bearing, but a perfect gentleness. The farmer
stands well on the world. Plain in manners as in
dress, he would not shine in palaces; he is abso-
lutely unknown and inadmissible therein; living or
dying, he never shall be heard of in them; yet the
drawing-room heroes put down beside him would
shrivel in his presence; he solid and unexpressive,
they expressed to gold-leaf. But he stands well on
the world, — as Adam did, as an Indian does, as
Homer's heroes, Agamemnon or Achilles, do. He
is a person whom a poet of any clime — Milton,
Firdusi, or Cervantes — would appreciate as being
really a piece of the old Nature, comparable to sun
and moon, rainbow and flood; because he is, as all
natural persons are, representative of Nature as
much as these.

That uncorrupted behavior which we admire in
animals and in young children belongs to him, to
the hunter, the sailor, — the man who lives in the
presence of Nature. Cities force growth and make
men talkative and entertaining, but they make
them artificial. What possesses interest for us is
the *naturel* of each, his constitutional excellence.
This is forever a surprise, engaging and lovely; we
cannot be satiated with knowing it, and about it;
and it is this which the conversation with Nature
cherishes and guards.

WORKS AND DAYS.

WORKS AND DAYS.

Our nineteenth century is the age of tools. They grow out of our structure. " Man is the meter of all things," said Aristotle ; " the hand is the instrument of instruments, and the mind is the form of forms." The human body is the magazine of inventions, the patent office, where are the models from which every hint was taken. All the tools and engines on earth are only extensions of its limbs and senses. One definition of man is " an intelligence served by organs." Machines can only second, not supply, his unaided senses. The body is a meter. The eye appreciates finer differences than art can expose. The apprentice clings to his foot-rule; a practised mechanic will measure by his thumb and his arm with equal precision; and a good surveyor will pace sixteen rods more accurately than another man can measure them by tape. The sympathy of eye and hand by which an Indian or a practised slinger hits his mark with a stone, or a wood-chopper or a carpenter swings his axe to a hair-line on his log, are examples ; and there is no

sense or organ which is not capable of exquisite
performance.

Men love to wonder, and that is the seed of our
science; and such is the mechanical determination
of our age, and so recent are our best contrivances,
that use has not dulled our joy and pride in them;
and we pity our fathers for dying before steam and
galvanism, sulphuric ether and ocean telegraphs,
photograph and spectroscope arrived, as cheated
out of half their human estate. These arts open
great gates of a future, promising to make the
world plastic and to lift human life out of its beg-
gary to a god-like ease and power.

Our century to be sure had inherited a tolerable
apparatus. We had the compass, the printing-
press, watches, the spiral spring, the barometer,
the telescope. Yet so many inventions have been
added that life seems almost made over new; and
as Leibnitz said of Newton, that "if he reckoned
all that had been done by mathematicians from the
beginning of the world down to Newton, and what
had been done by him, his would be the better
half," so one might say that the inventions of the
last fifty years counterpoise those of the fifty centuries before them. For the vast production and
manifold application of iron is new; and our common and indispensable utensils of house and farm
are new; the sewing-machine, the power-loom, the

McCormick reaper, the mowing-machines, gas-light, lucifer matches, and the immense productions of the laboratory, are new in this century, and one franc's worth of coal does the work of a laborer for twenty days.

Why need I speak of steam, the enemy of space and time, with its enormous strength and delicate applicability, which is made in hospitals to bring a bowl of gruel to a sick man's bed, and can twist beams of iron like candy-braids, and vies with the forces which upheaved and doubled over the geologic strata? Steam is an apt scholar and a strong-shouldered fellow, but it has not yet done all its work. It already walks about the field like a man, and will do anything required of it. It irrigates crops, and drags away a mountain. It must sew our shirts, it must drive our gigs; taught by Mr. Babbage, it must calculate interest and logarithms. Lord Chancellor Thurlow thought it might be made to draw bills and answers in chancery. If that were satire, it is yet coming to render many higher services of a mechanico-intellectual kind, and will leave the satire short of the fact.

How excellent are the mechanical aids we have applied to the human body, as in dentistry, in vaccination, in the rhinoplastic treatment; in the beautiful aid of ether, like a finer sleep; and in the boldest promiser of all, — the transfusion of the

blood, — which, in Paris, it was claimed, enables a
man to change his blood as often as his linen !

What of this dapper caoutchouc and gutta-percha, which make water-pipes and stomach-pumps,
belting for mill-wheels, and diving bells, and rain-
proof coats for all climates, which teach us to defy
the wet, and put every man on a footing with the
beaver and the crocodile? What of the grand tools
with which we engineer, like kobolds and enchant-
ers, tunnelling Alps, canalling the American Isth-
mus, piercing the Arabian desert? In Massachusetts we fight the sea successfully with beach-grass
and broom, and the blowing sand-barrens with pine
plantations. The soil of Holland, once the most
populous in Europe, is below the level of the sea.
Egypt, where no rain fell for three thousand years,
now, it is said, thanks Mehemet Ali's irrigations
and planted forests for late-returning showers.
The old Hebrew king said, " He makes the wrath
of man to praise him." And there is no argument
of theism better than the grandeur of ends brought
about by paltry means. The chain of Western
railroads from Chicago to the Pacific has planted
cities and civilization in less time than it costs to
bring an orchard into bearing.

What shall we say of the ocean telegraph, that
extension of the eye and ear, whose sudden performance astonished mankind as if the intellect

were taking the brute earth itself into training, and shooting the first thrills of life and thought through the unwilling brain?

There does not seem any limit to these new informations of the same Spirit that made the elements at first, and now, through man, works them. Art and power will go on as they have done, — will make day out of night, time out of space, and space out of time.

Invention breeds invention. No sooner is the electric telegraph devised than gutta-percha, the very material it requires, is found. The aeronaut is provided with gun-cotton, the very fuel he wants for his balloon. When commerce is vastly enlarged, California and Australia expose the gold it needs. When Europe is over-populated, America and Australia crave to be peopled; and so throughout, every chance is timed, as if Nature, who made the lock, knew where to find the key.

Another result of our arts is the new intercourse which is surprising us with new solutions of the embarrassing political problems. The intercourse is not new, but the scale is new. Our selfishness would have held slaves or would have excluded from a quarter of the planet all that are not born on the soil of that quarter. Our politics are disgusting; but what can they help or hinder when from time to time the primal instincts are im-

pressed on masses of mankind, when the nations
are in exodus and flux ? Nature loves to cross her
stocks, — and German, Chinese, Turk, Russ, and
Kanaka were putting out to sea, and intermarry-
ing race with race; and commerce took the hint,
and ships were built capacious enough to carry the
people of a county.

This thousand-handed art has introduced a new
element into the state. The science of power is
forced to remember the power of science. Civilization mounts and climbs. Malthus, when he stated
that the mouths went on multiplying geometrically
and the food only arithmetically, forgot to say that
the human mind was also a factor in political economy, and that the augmenting wants of society
would be met by an augmenting power of invention.

Yes, we have a pretty artillery of tools now in
our social arrangements : we ride four times as fast
as our fathers did ; travel, grind, weave, forge,
plant, till, and excavate better. We have new
shoes, gloves, glasses, and gimlets ; we have the cal-
culus ; we have the newspaper, which does its best
to make every square acre of land and sea give an
account of itself at your breakfast-table ; we have
money, and paper money : we have language, —
the finest tool of all, and nearest to the mind.
Much will have more. Man flatters himself that

his command over nature must increase. Things begin to obey him. We are to have the balloon yet, and the next war will be fought in the air. We may yet find a rose water that will wash the negro white. He sees the skull of the English race changing from its Saxon type under the exigencies of American life.

Tantalus, who in old times was seen vainly trying to quench his thirst with a flowing stream which ebbed whenever he approached it, has been seen again lately. He is in Paris, in New York, in Boston. He is now in great spirits; thinks he shall reach it yet; thinks he shall bottle the wave. It is however getting a little doubtful. Things have an ugly look still. No matter how many centuries of culture have preceded, the new man always finds himself standing on the brink of chaos, always in a crisis. Can anybody remember when the times were not hard, and money not scarce? Can anybody remember when sensible men, and the right sort of men, and the right sort of women, were plentiful? Tantalus begins to think steam a delusion, and galvanism no better than it should be.

Many facts concur to show that we must look deeper for our salvation than to steam, photographs, balloons or astronomy. These tools have some questionable properties. They are reagents. Machinery is aggressive. The weaver becomes a web, the machinist a machine. If you do not use the tools, they use you. All tools are in one sense edge-tools, and dangerous. A man builds a fine house; and now he has a master, and a task for life: he is to furnish, watch, show it, and keep it in repair, the rest of his days. A man has a reputation, and is no longer free, but must respect that. A man makes a picture or a book, and, if it succeeds, 't is often the worse for him. I saw a brave man the other day, hitherto as free as the hawk or the fox of the wilderness, constructing his cabinet of drawers for shells, eggs, minerals, and mounted birds. It was easy to see that he was amusing himself with making pretty links for his own limbs.

Then the political economist thinks " 't is doubtful if all the mechanical inventions that ever existed have lightened the day's toil of one human being." The machine unmakes the man. Now that the machine is so perfect, the engineer is nobody. Every new step in improving the engine restricts one more act of the engineer, — unteaches him. Once it took Archimedes; now it only needs a fireman, and a boy to know the coppers, to pull up the handles or mind the water-tank. But when the engine breaks, they can do nothing.

What sickening details in the daily journals! I

believe they have ceased to publish the "Newgate
Calendar" and the "Pirate's Own Book" since the
family newspapers, namely the "New York Tribune" and the "London Times" have quite super-
seded them in the freshness as well as the horror of
their records of crime. Politics were never more
corrupt and brutal; and Trade, that pride and darling of our ocean, that educator of nations, that benefactor in spite of itself, ends in shameful default-
ing, bubble, and bankruptcy, all over the world.

Of course we resort to the enumeration of his
arts and inventions as a measure of the worth of
man. But if, with all his arts, he is a felon, we
cannot assume the mechanical skill or chemical resources as the measure of worth. Let us try another
gauge.

What have these arts done for the character, for
the worth of mankind? Are men better? 'T is
sometimes questioned whether morals have not declined as the arts have ascended. Here are great
arts and little men. Here is greatness begotten of
paltriness. We cannot trace the triumphs of civilization to such benefactors as we wish. The greatest meliorator of the world is selfish, huckstering
Trade. Every victory over matter ought to recommend to man the worth of his nature. But now
one wonders who did all this good. Look up the
inventors. Each has his own knack; his genius is

in veins and spots. But the great, equal, sym-
metrical brain, fed from a great heart, you shall not
find. Every one has more to hide than he has to
show, or is lamed by his excellence. 'T is too
plain that with the material power the moral progress has not kept pace. It appears that we have
not made a judicious investment. Works and days
were offered us, and we took works.

The new study of the Sanskrit has shown us the
origin of the old names of God, — Dyaus, Deus,
Zeus, Zeu pater, Jupiter, — names of the sun, still
recognizable through the modifications of our ver-
nacular words, importing that the Day is the Divine Power and Manifestation, and indicating that
those ancient men, in their attempts to express
the Supreme Power of the universe, called him the
Day, and that this name was accepted by all the
tribes.

Hesiod wrote a poem which he called "Works
and Days," in which he marked the changes of the
Greek year, instructing the husbandman at the rising of what constellation he might safely sow, when
to reap, when to gather wood, when the sailor
might launch his boat in security from storms, and
what admonitions of the planets he must heed. It
is full of economies for Grecian life, noting the
proper age for marriage, the rules of household
thrift, and of hospitality. The poem is full of piety

as well as prudence, and is adapted to all merid-
ians by adding the ethics of works and of days.
But he has not pushed his study of days into such
inquiry and analysis as they invite.

A farmer said " he should like to have all the
land that joined his own." Bonaparte, who had the
same appetite, endeavored to make the Mediter-
ranean a French lake. Czar Alexander was more
expansive, and wished to call the Pacific *my ocean ;*
and the Americans were obliged to resist his attempts to make it a close sea. But if he had the
earth for his pasture and the sea for his pond he
would be a pauper still. He only is rich who owns
the day. There is no king, rich man, fairy, or
demon who possesses such power as that. The days
are ever divine as to the first Aryans. They are
of the least pretension and of the greatest capacity
of anything that exists. They come and go like
muffled and veiled figures, sent from a distant
friendly party ; but they say nothing, and if we do
not use the gifts they bring, they carry them as
silently away.

How the day fits itself to the mind, winds itself
round it like a fine drapery, clothing all its fancies !
Any holiday communicates to us its color. We
wear its cockade and favors in our humor. Remember what boys think in the morning of " Election day," of the Fourth of July, of Thanksgiving

or Christmas. The very stars in their courses wink to them of nuts and cakes, bonbons, presents, and fire-works. Cannot memory still descry the old school-house and its porch, somewhat hacked by jack-knives, where you spun tops and snapped marbles; and do you not recall that life was then calendared by moments, threw itself into nervous knots of glittering hours, even as now, and not spread itself abroad an equable felicity? In college terms, and in years that followed, the young graduate, when the Commencement anniversary returned, though he were in a swamp, would see a festive light and find the air faintly echoing with plausive academic thunders. In solitude and in the country, what dignity distinguishes the holy time! The old Sabbath, or Seventh Day, white with the religions of unknown thousands of years, when this hallowed hour dawns out of the deep, — a clean page, which the wise may inscribe with truth, whilst the savage scrawls it with fetishes, — the cathedral music of history breathes through it a psalm to our solitude.

So, in the common experience of the scholar, the weathers fit his moods. A thousand tunes the variable wind plays, a thousand spectacles it brings, and each is the frame or dwelling of a new spirit. I used formerly to choose my time with some nicety for each favorite book. One author is good for

winter, and one for the dog-days. The scholar
must look long for the right hour for Plato's Timæus. At last the elect morning arrives, the early
dawn, — a few lights conspicuous in the heaven, as
of a world just created and still becoming, — and
in its wide leisures we dare open that book.

There are days when the great are near us, when
there is no frown on their brow, no condescension
even; when they take us by the hand, and we share
their thought. There are days which are the car-
nival of the year. The angels assume flesh, and
repeatedly become visible. The imagination of the
gods is excited and rushes on every side into forms.
Yesterday not a bird peeped; the world was barren,
peaked, and pining: to-day 't is inconceivably populous; creation swarms and meliorates.

The days are made on a loom whereof the warp
and woof are past and future time. They are
majestically dressed, as if every god brought a
thread to the skyey web. 'T is pitiful the things
by which we are rich or poor, — a matter of coins,
coats, and carpets, a little more or less stone, or
wood, or paint, the fashion of a cloak or hat; like
the luck of naked Indians, of whom one is proud
in the possession of a glass bead or a red feather,
and the rest miserable in the want of it. But the
treasures which Nature spent itself to amass, — the
secular, refined, composite anatomy of man, which

all strata go to form, which the prior races, from infusory and saurian, existed to ripen; the surrounding plastic natures; the earth with its foods; the intellectual, temperamenting air; the sea with its invitations; the heaven deep with worlds; and the answering brain and nervous structure replying to these; the eye that looketh into the deeps, which again look back to the eye, abyss to abyss; — these, not like a glass bead, or the coins or carpets, are given immeasurably to all.

This miracle is hurled into every beggar's hands. The blue sky is a covering for a market and for the cherubim and seraphim. The sky is the varnish or glory with which the Artist has washed the whole work, — the verge or confines of matter and spirit. Nature could no farther go. Could our happiest dream come to pass in solid fact, — could a power open our eyes to behold "millions of spiritual creatures walk the earth," — I believe I should find that mid-plain on which they moved floored beneath and arched above with the same web of blue depth which weaves itself over me now, as I trudge the streets on my affairs.

It is singular that our rich English language should have no word to denote the face of the world. *Kinde* was the old English term, which, however, filled only half the range of our fine Latin word, with its delicate future tense,— *natura, about to be born*, or what German philosophy denotes as a *becoming*. But nothing expresses that power which seems to work for beauty alone. The Greek *Kosmos* did; and therefore, with great propriety, Humboldt entitles his book, which recounts the last results of science, *Cosmos*.

Such are the days, — the earth is the cup, the sky is the cover, of the immense bounty of nature which is offered us for our daily aliment; but what a force of *illusion* begins life with us and attends us to the end! We are coaxed, flattered, and duped, from morn to eve, from birth to death; and where is the old eye that ever saw through the deception? The Hindoos represent Maia, the illusory energy of Vishnu, as one of his principal attributes. As if, in this gale of warring elements which life is, it was necessary to bind souls to human life as mariners in a tempest lash themselves to the mast and bulwarks of a ship, and Nature employed certain illusions as her ties and straps, — a rattle, a doll, an apple, for a child; skates, a river, a boat, a horse, a gun, for the growing boy; and I will not begin to name those of the youth and adult, for they are numberless. Seldom and slowly the mask falls and the pupil is permitted to see that all is one stuff, cooked and painted under many counterfeit appearances. Hume's doctrine was that the circumstances vary, the amount of

happiness does not: that the beggar cracking fleas
in the sunshine under a hedge, and the duke rolling by in his chariot; the girl equipped for her first
ball, and the orator returning triumphant from the
debate, had different means, but the same quantity
of pleasant excitement.

This element of illusion lends all its force to hide
the values of present time. Who is he that does
not always find himself doing something less than
his best task? "What are you doing?" "O,
nothing; I have been doing thus, or I shall do so
or so, but now I am only —" Ah! poor dupe,
will you never slip out of the web of the master
juggler, — never learn that as soon as the irrecov-
erable years have woven their blue glory between
to-day and us these passing hours shall glitter and
draw us as the wildest romance and the homes of
beauty and poetry? How difficult to deal erect
with them! The events they bring, their trade,
entertainments, and gossip, their urgent work, all
throw dust in the eyes and distract attention. He
is a strong man who can look them in the eye, see
through this juggle, feel their identity, and keep
his own; who can know surely that one will be like
another to the end of the world, nor permit love, or
death, or politics, or money, war, or pleasure, to
draw him from his task.

The world is always equal to itself, and every

man in moments of deeper thought is apprised that
he is repeating the experiences of the people in the
streets of Thebes or Byzantium. An everlasting
Now reigns in nature, which hangs the same roses
on our bushes which charmed the Roman and the
Chaldæan in their hanging gardens. 'To what
end, then,' he asks, ' should I study languages, and
traverse countries, to learn so simple truths?'

History of ancient art, excavated cities, recovery
of books and inscriptions, — yes, the works were
beautiful, and the history worth knowing; and
academies convene to settle the claims of the old
schools. What journeys and measurements, — Niebuhr and Müller and Layard, — to identify the
plain of Troy and Nimroud town! And your homage to Dante costs you so much sailing; and to
ascertain the discoverers of America needs as much
voyaging as the discovery cost. Poor child! that
flexile clay of which these old brothers moulded
their admirable symbols was not Persian, nor Mem-
phian, nor Teutonic, nor local at all, but was common lime and silex and water and sunlight, the heat
of the blood and the heaving of the lungs; it was
that clay which thou heldest but now in thy foolish
hands, and threwest away to go and seek in vain
in sepulchres, mummy-pits, and old book-shops of
Asia Minor, Egypt, and England. It was the
deep to-day which all men scorn; the rich poverty

which men hate; the populous, all-loving solitude
which men quit for the tattle of towns. He lurks,
he hides, — *he* who is success, reality, joy, and
power. One of the illusions is that the present
hour is not the critical, decisive hour. Write it on
your heart that every day is the best day in the
year. No man has learned anything rightly until
he knows that every day is Doomsday. 'T is the
old secret of the gods that they come in low disguises. 'T is the vulgar great who come dizened
with gold and jewels. Real kings hide away their
crowns in their wardrobes, and affect a plain and
poor exterior. In the Norse legend of our ancestors, Odin dwells in a fisher's hut and patches
a boat. In the Hindoo legends, Hari dwells a
peasant among peasants. In the Greek legend,
Apollo lodges with the shepherds of Admetus, and
Jove liked to rusticate among the poor Ethiopians.
So, in our history, Jesus is born in a barn, and his
twelve peers are fishermen. 'T is the very principle
of science that Nature shows herself best in leasts;
it was the maxim of Aristotle and Lucretius; and,
in modern times, of Swedenborg and of Hahne-
mann. The order of changes in the egg deter-
mines the age of fossil strata. So it was the rule
of our poets, in the legends of fairy lore, that the
fairies largest in power were the least in size. In
the Christian graces, humility stands highest of all,

in the form of the Madonna ; and in life, this is
the secret of the wise. We owe to genius always
the same debt, of lifting the curtain from the common, and showing us that divinities are sitting disguised in the seeming gang of gypsies and pedlers.
In daily life, what distinguishes the master is the
using those materials he has, instead of looking
about for what are more renowned, or what others
have used well. " A general," said Bonaparte,
" always has troops enough, if he only knows how
to employ those he has, and bivouacs with them."
Do not refuse the employment which the hour
brings you, for one more ambitious. The highest
heaven of wisdom is alike near from every point,
and thou must find it, if at all, by methods native
to thyself alone.

That work is ever the more pleasant to the imagination which is not now required. How wistfully,
when we have promised to attend the working
committee, we look at the distant hills and their
seductions !

The use of history is to give value to the present
hour and its duty. That is good which commends
to me my country, my climate, my means and materials, my associates. I knew a man in a certain
religious exaltation who " thought it an honor to
wash his own face." He seemed to me more sane
than those who hold themselves cheap.

Zoölogists may deny that horse-hairs in the water change to worms, but I find that whatever is old corrupts, and the past turns to snakes. The reverence for the deeds of our ancestors is a treacherous sentiment. Their merit was not to reverence the old, but to honor the present moment; and we falsely make them excuses of the very habit which they hated and defied.

Another illusion is that there is not time enough for our work. Yet we might reflect that though many creatures eat from one dish, each, according to its constitution, assimilates from the elements what belongs to it, whether time, or space, or light, or water, or food. A snake converts whatever prey the meadow yields him into snake; a fox, into fox; and Peter and John are working up all existence into Peter and John. A poor Indian chief of the Six Nations of New York made a wiser reply than any philosopher, to some one complaining that he had not enough time. " Well," said Red Jacket, " I suppose you have all there is."

A third illusion haunts us, that a long duration, as a year, a decade, a century, is valuable. But an old French sentence says, " God works in moments," — " *En peu d'heure Dieu labeure.*" We ask for long life, but 't is deep life, or grand moments, that signify. Let the measure of time be spiritual, not mechanical. Life is unnecessarily long. Moments of insight, of fine personal relation, a smile, a glance, — what ample borrowers of eternity they are! Life culminates and concentrates; and Homer said, " The gods ever give to mortals their apportioned share of reason only on one day."

I am of the opinion of the poet Wordsworth, that " there is no real happiness in this life but in intellect and virtue." I am of the opinion of Pliny, that " whilst we are musing on these things, we are adding to the length of our lives." I am of the opinion of Glauco, who said, " The measure of life, O Socrates, is, with the wise, the speaking and hearing such discourses as yours."

He only can enrich me who can recommend to me the space between sun and sun. 'T is the measure of a man, — his apprehension of a day. For we do not listen with the best regard to the verses of a man who is only a poet, nor to his problems if he is only an algebraist; but if a man is at once acquainted with the geometric foundations of things and with their festal splendor, his poetry is exact and his arithmetic musical. And him I reckon the most learned scholar, not who can unearth for me the buried dynasties of Sesostris and Ptolemy, the Sothiac era, the Olympiads and consulships, but who can unfold the theory of this particular Wednesday. Can he uncover the ligaments concealed

from all but piety, which attach the dull men and
things we know to the First Cause? These passing fifteen minutes, men think, are time, not eternity; are low and subaltern, are but hope or memory; that is, the way *to* or the way *from* welfare,
but not welfare. Can. he show their tie? That
interpreter shall guide us from a menial and elee-
mosynary existence into riches and stability. He
dignifies the place where he is. This mendicant
America, this curious, peering, itinerant, imitative
America, studious of Greece and Rome, of England and Germany, will take off its dusty shoes,
will take off its glazed traveller's-cap and sit at
home with repose and deep joy on its face. The
world has no such landscape, the æons of history
no such hour, the future no equal second opportunity. Now let poets sing! now let arts unfold!

One more view remains. But life is good only
when it is magical and musical, a perfect timing
and consent, and when we do not anatomize it.
You must treat the days respectfully, you must be
a day yourself, and not interrogate it like a college
professor. The world is enigmatical, — everything
said, and everything known or done, — and must
not be taken literally, but genially. We must be
at the top of our condition to understand anything
rightly. You must hear the bird's song without
attempting to render it into nouns and verbs. Can-

not we be a little abstemious and obedient? Cannot we let the morning be?

Everything in the universe goes by indirection. There are no straight lines. I remember well the foreign scholar who made a week of my youth happy by his visit. "The savages in the islands," he said, "delight to play with the surf, coming in on the top of the rollers, then swimming out again, and repeat the delicious manœuvre for hours. Well, human life is made up of such transits. There can be no greatness without abandonment. But here your very astronomy is an espionage. I dare not go out of doors and see the moon and stars, but they seem to measure my tasks, to ask how many lines or pages are finished since I saw them last. Not so, as I told you, was it in Belleisle. The days at Belleisle were all different, and only joined by a perfect love of the same object. Just to fill the hour, — that is happiness. Fill my hour, ye gods, so that I shall not say, whilst I have done this, 'Behold, also, an hour of my life is gone,' — but rather, 'I have lived an hour.'"

We do not want factitious men, who can do any literary or professional feat, as, to write poems, or advocate a cause, or carry a measure, for money; or turn their ability indifferently in any particular direction by the strong effort of will. No, what has been best done in the world, — the works of genius, — cost nothing. There is no painful effort, but it is the spontaneous flowing of the thought. Shakspeare made his Hamlet as a bird weaves its nest. Poems have been written between sleeping and waking, irresponsibly. Fancy defines herself :

> " Forms that men spy
> With the half-shut eye
> In the beams of the setting sun, am I."

The masters painted for joy, and knew not that virtue had gone out of them. They could not paint the like in cold blood. The masters of English lyric wrote their songs so. It was a fine efflorescence of fine powers ; as was said of the letters of the Frenchwoman, — " the charming accident of their more charming existence." Then the poet is never the poorer for his song. A song is no song unless the circumstance is free and fine. If the singer sing from a sense of duty or from seeing no way of escape, I had rather have none. Those only can sleep who do not care to sleep ; and those only write or speak best who do not too much respect the writing or the speaking.

The same rule holds in science. The savant is often an amateur. His performance is a memoir to the Academy on fish-worms, tadpoles, or spiders' legs ; he observes as other academicians observe ; he is on stilts at a microscope, and his memoir finished and read and printed, he retreats into his routinary existence, which is quite separate from his scientific. But in Newton, science was as easy as breathing; he used the same wit to weigh the moon that he used to buckle his shoes; and all his life was simple, wise, and majestic. So was it in Archimedes, — always self-same, like the sky. In Linnæus, in Franklin, the like sweetness and equality, — no stilts, no tiptoe; and their results are wholesome and memorable to all men.

In stripping time of its illusions, in seeking to find what is the heart of the day, we come to the quality of the moment, and drop the duration altogether. It is the depth at which we live and not at all the surface extension that imports. We pierce to the eternity, of which time is the flitting surface; and, really, the least acceleration of thought and the least increase of power of thought, make life to seem and to be of vast duration. We call it time; but when that acceleration and that deepening take effect, it acquires another and a higher name.

There are people who do not need much experimenting; who, after years of activity, say, We knew all this before; who love at first sight and hate at first sight; discern the affinities and repulsions; who do not care so much for conditions as others, for they are always in one condition and enjoy themselves; who dictate to others and are

not dictated to ; who in their consciousness of de-
serving success constantly slight the ordinary means
of attaining it; who have self-existence and self-
help ; who are suffered to be themselves in society ;
who are great in the present ; who have no talents,
or care not to have them, — being that which was
before talent, and shall be after it, and of which
talent seems only a tool: this is character, the
highest name at which philosophy has arrived.

'T is not important how the hero does this or this,
but what he is.   What he is will appear in every
gesture and syllable.   In this way the moment and
the character are one.

It is a fine fable for the advantage of character
over talent, the Greek legend of the strife of Jove
and Phœbus.   Phœbus challenged the gods, and
said, " Who will outshoot the far-darting Apollo ? "
Zeus said, " I will."   Mars shook the lots in his
helmet, and that of Apollo leaped out first.   Apollo
stretched his bow and shot his arrow into the extreme west.   Then Zeus arose, and with one stride
cleared the whole distance, and said, " Where shall
I shoot? there is no space left."   So the bowman's
prize was adjudged to him who drew no bow.

And this is the progress of every earnest mind ;
from the works of man and the activity of the
hands to a delight in the faculties which rule them ;
from a respect to the works to a wise wonder at this

mystic element of time in which he is conditioned; from local skills and the economy which reckons the amount of production *per* hour to the finer economy which respects the quality of what is done, and the right we have to the work, or the fidelity with which it flows from ourselves; then to the depth of thought it betrays, looking to its universality, or that its roots are in eternity, not in time. Then it flows from character, that sublime health which values one moment as another, and makes us great in all conditions, and as the only definition we have of freedom and power.

BOOKS.

BOOKS.

It is easy to accuse books, and bad ones are easily found; and the best are but records, and not the things recorded; and certainly there is dilettanteism enough, and books that are merely neutral and do nothing for us. In Plato's Gorgias, Socrates says: "The shipmaster walks in a modest garb near the sea, after bringing his passengers from Ægina or from Pontus; not thinking he has done anything extraordinary, and certainly knowing that his passengers are the same and in no respect better than when he took them on board." So is it with books, for the most part: they work no redemption in us. The bookseller might certainly know that his customers are in no respect better for the purchase and consumption of his wares. The volume is dear at a dollar, and after reading to weariness the lettered backs, we leave the shop with a sigh, and learn, as I did without surprise of a surly bank director, that in bank parlors they estimate all stocks of this kind as rubbish.

But it is not less true that there are books which are of that importance in a man's private experience as to verify for him the fables of Cornelius Agrippa, of Michael Scott, or of the old Orpheus of Thrace, — books which take rank in our life with parents and lovers and passionate experiences, so medicinal, so stringent, so revolutionary, so authoritative, — books which are the work and the proof of faculties so comprehensive, so nearly equal to the world which they paint, that though one shuts them with meaner ones, he feels his exclusion from them to accuse his way of living.

Consider what you have in the smallest chosen library. A company of the wisest and wittiest men that could be picked out of all civil countries in a thousand years have set in best order the results of their learning and wisdom. The men themselves were hid and inaccessible, solitary, impatient of interruption, fenced by etiquette; but the thought which they did not uncover to their bosom friend is here written out in transparent words to us, the strangers of another age.

We owe to books those general benefits which come from high intellectual action. Thus, I think, we often owe to them the perception of immortality. They impart sympathetic activity to the moral power. Go with mean people and you think life is mean. Then read Plutarch, and the world is a

proud place, peopled with men of positive quality,
with heroes and demigods standing around us, who
will not let us sleep. Then, they address the imagination : only poetry inspires poetry. They become
the organic culture of the time. College education
is the reading of certain books which the common
sense of all scholars agrees will represent the science already accumulated. If you know that, —
for instance in geometry, if you have read Euclid
and Laplace, — your opinion has some value; if
you do not know these, you are not entitled to give
any opinion on the subject. Whenever any skeptic or bigot claims to be heard on the questions of
intellect and morals, we ask if he is familiar with
the books of Plato, where all his pert objections
have once for all been disposed of. If not, he has
no right to our time. Let him go and find himself
answered there.

Meantime the colleges, whilst they provide us
with libraries, furnish no professor of books ; and
I think no chair is so much wanted. In a library
we are surrounded by many hundreds of dear
friends, but they are imprisoned by an enchanter
in these paper and leathern boxes ; and though they
know us, and have been waiting two, ten, or twenty
centuries for us, — some of them, — and are eager
to give us a sign and unbosom themselves, it is the
law of their limbo that they must not speak until

spoken to ; and as the enchanter has dressed them,
like battalions of infantry, in coat and jacket of
one cut, by the thousand and ten thousand, your
chance of hitting on the right one is to be com-
puted by the arithmetical rule of Permutation and
Combination, — not a choice out of three caskets,
but out of half a million caskets, all alike. But it
happens in our experience that in this lottery there
are at least fifty or a hundred blanks to a prize.
It seems then as if some charitable soul, after losing
a great deal of time among the false books and
alighting upon a few true ones which made him
happy and wise, would do a right act in naming
those which have been bridges or ships to carry
him safely over dark morasses and barren oceans,
into the heart of sacred cities, into palaces and
temples. This would be best done by those great
masters of books who from time to time appear, —
the Fabricii, the Seldens, Magliabecchis, Scaligers,
Mirandolas, Bayles, Johnsons, whose eyes sweep
the whole horizon of learning. But private readers,
reading purely for love of the book, would serve
us by leaving each the shortest note of what he
found.

There are books; and it is practicable to read
them, because they are so few. We look over with
a sigh the monumental libraries of Paris, of the
Vatican, and the British Museum. In 1858, the

number of printed books in the Imperial Library
at Paris was estimated at eight hundred thousand
volumes, with an annual increase of twelve thousand volumes; so that the number of printed books
extant to-day may easily exceed a million. It is
easy to count the number of pages which a diligent
man can read in a day, and the number of years
which human life in favorable circumstances allows
to reading; and to demonstrate that though he
should read from dawn till dark, for sixty years,
he must die in the first alcoves. But nothing can
be more deceptive than this arithmetic, where none
but a natural method is really pertinent. I visit
occasionally the Cambridge Library, and I can
seldom go there without renewing the conviction
that the best of it all is already within the four
walls of my study at home. The inspection of the
catalogue brings me continually back to the few
standard writers who are on every private shelf;
and to these it can afford only the most slight and
casual additions. The crowds and centuries of
books are only commentary and elucidation, echoes
and weakeners of these few great voices of time.

The best rule of reading will be a method from
nature, and not a mechanical one of hours and
pages. It holds each student to a pursuit of his
native aim, instead of a desultory miscellany. Let
him read what is proper to him, and not waste his

memory on a crowd of mediocrities.   As whole
nations have derived their culture from a single
book, — as the Bible has been the literature as
well as the religion of large portions of Europe ; as
Hafiz was the eminent genius of the Persians, Confucius of the Chinese, Cervantes of the Spaniards ;
so, perhaps, the human mind would be a gainer
if all the secondary writers were lost, — say, in
England, all but Shakspeare, Milton, and Bacon,
— through the profounder study so drawn to those
wonderful minds.   With this pilot of his own
genius, let the student read one, or let him read
many, he will read advantageously.   Dr. Johnson
said : " Whilst you stand deliberating which book
your son shall read first, another boy has read both:
read anything five hours a day, and you will soon
be learned."

Nature is much our friend in this matter.   Nature
is always clarifying her water and her wine.   No
filtration can be so perfect.   She does the same
thing by books as by her gases and plants.   There
is always a selection in writers, and then a selection
from the selection.   In the first place, all books
that get fairly into the vital air of the world were
written by the successful class, by the affirming and
advancing class, who utter what tens of thousands
feel though they cannot say.   There has already
been a scrutiny and choice from many hundreds of

young pens before the pamphlet or political chapter which you read in a fugitive journal comes to your eye. All these are young adventurers, who produce their performance to the wise ear of Time, who sits and weighs, and, ten years hence, out of a million of pages reprints one. Again it is judged, it is winnowed by all the winds of opinion, and what terrific selection has not passed on it before it can be reprinted after twenty years; — and reprinted after a century! — it is as if Minos and Rhadamanthus had indorsed the writing. 'T is therefore an economy of time to read old and famed books. Nothing can be preserved which is not good; and I know beforehand that Pindar, Martial, Terence, Galen, Kepler, Galileo, Bacon, Erasmus, More, will be superior to the average intellect. In contemporaries, it is not so easy to distinguish betwixt notoriety and fame.

Be sure then to read no mean books. Shun the spawn of the press on the gossip of the hour. Do not read what you shall learn, without asking, in the street and the train. Dr. Johnson said "he always went into stately shops;" and good travellers stop at the best hotels; for though they cost more, they do not cost much more, and there is the good company and the best information. In like manner the scholar knows that the famed books contain, first and last, the best thoughts and facts.

Now and then, by rarest luck, in some foolish Grub Street is the gem we want. But in the best circles is the best information. If you should transfer the amount of your reading day by day from the newspaper to the standard authors —— But who dare speak of such a thing?

The three practical rules, then, which I have to offer, are, — 1. Never read any book that is not a year old. 2. Never read any but famed books. 3. Never read any but what you like ; or, in Shakspeare's phrase, —

> "No profit goes where is no pleasure ta'en :
> In brief, sir, study what you most affect."

Montaigne says, "Books are a languid pleasure ; " but I find certain books vital and spermatic, not leaving the reader what he was : he shuts the book a richer man. I would never willingly read any others than such. And I will venture, at the risk of inditing a list of old primers and grammars, to count the few books which a superficial reader must thankfully use.

Of the old Greek books, I think there are five which we cannot spare : 1. Homer, who in spite of Pope and all the learned uproar of centuries, has really the true fire and is good for simple minds, is the true and adequate germ of Greece, and occupies that place as history which nothing can supply. It

holds through all literature that our best history is
still poetry. It is so in Hebrew, in Sanskrit, and
in Greek. English history is best known through
Shakspeare; how much through Merlin, Robin
Hood, and the Scottish ballads! — the German,
through the Nibelungenlied; — the Spanish, through
the Cid. Of Homer, George Chapman's is the heroic translation, though the most literal prose version is the best of all. 2. Herodotus, whose history
contains inestimable anecdotes, which brought it
with the learned into a sort of disesteem; but in
these days, when it is found that what is most memorable of history is a few anecdotes, and that we
need not be alarmed though we should find it not
dull, it is regaining credit. 3. Æschylus, the grandest of the three tragedians, who has given us under
a thin veil the first plantation of Europe. The
" Prometheus " is a poem of the like dignity and
scope as the Book of Job, or the Norse Edda.
4. Of Plato I hesitate to speak, lest there should
be no end. You find in him that which you have
already found in Homer, now ripened to thought,
— the poet converted to a philosopher, with loftier
strains of musical wisdom than Homer reached; as
if Homer were the youth and Plato the finished
man; yet with no less security of bold and perfect
song, when he cares to use it, and with some harp-
strings fetched from a higher heaven. He contains

the future, as he came out of the past. In Plato
you explore modern Europe in its causes and seed,
— all that in thought, which the history of Europe
embodies or has yet to embody. The well-informed
man finds himself anticipated. Plato is up with
him too. Nothing has escaped him. Every new
crop in the fertile harvest of reform, every fresh
suggestion of modern humanity, is there. If the
student wish to see both sides, and justice done
to the man of the world, pitiless exposure of ped-
ants, and the supremacy of truth and the religious
sentiment, he shall be contented also. Why should
not young men be educated on this book? It
would suffice for the tuition of the race; to test
their understanding, and to express their reason.
Here is that which is so attractive to all men, —
the literature of aristocracy shall I call it? — the
picture of the best persons, sentiments, and manners, by the first master, in the best times; portraits
of Pericles, Alcibiades, Crito, Prodicus, Protagoras,
Anaxagoras, and Socrates, with the lovely back-
ground of the Athenian and suburban landscape.
Or who can overestimate the images with which
Plato has enriched the minds of men, and which
pass like bullion in the currency of all nations?
Read the " Phædo," the " Protagoras," the " Phæ-
drus," the " Timæus," the " Republic," and the
" Apology of Socrates." 5. Plutarch cannot be

spared from the smallest library; first because he is so readable, which is much; then that he is medicinal and invigorating. The lives of Cimon, Lycurgus, Alexander, Demosthenes, Phocion, Marcellus, and the rest, are what history has of best. But this book has taken care of itself, and the opinion of the world is expressed in the innumerable cheap editions, which make it as accessible as a newspaper. But Plutarch's "Morals" is less known, and seldom reprinted. Yet such a reader as I am writing to can as ill spare it as the "Lives." He will read in it the essays "On the Dæmon of Socrates," "On Isis and Osiris," "On Progress in Virtue," "On Garrulity," "On Love;" and thank anew the art of printing and the cheerful domain of ancient thinking. Plutarch charms by the facility of his associations; so that it signifies little where you open his book, you find yourself at the Olympian tables. His memory is like the Isthmian Games, where all that was excellent in Greece was assembled; and you are stimulated and recruited by lyric verses, by philosophic sentiments, by the forms and behavior of heroes, by the worship of the gods, and by the passing of fillets, parsley and laurel wreaths, chariots, armor, sacred cups, and utensils of sacrifice. An inestimable trilogy of ancient social pictures are the three "Banquets" respectively of Plato, Xenophon, and Plutarch.

Plutarch's has the least approach to historical accuracy; but the meeting of the Seven Wise Masters is a charming portraiture of ancient manners and discourse, and is as clear as the voice of a fife, and entertaining as a French novel. Xenophon's delineation of Athenian manners is an accessory to Plato, and supplies traits of Socrates; whilst Plato's has merits of every kind, — being a repertory of the wisdom of the ancients on the subject of love; a picture of a feast of wits, not less descriptive than Aristophanes; and, lastly, containing that ironical eulogy of Socrates which is the source from which all the portraits of that philosopher current in Europe have been drawn.

Of course a certain outline should be obtained of Greek history, in which the important moments and persons can be rightly set down; but the shortest is the best, and if one lacks stomach for Mr. Grote's voluminous annals, the old slight and popular summary of Goldsmith or of Gillies will serve. The valuable part is the age of Pericles and the next generation. And here we must read the " Clouds " of Aristophanes, and what more of that master we gain appetite for, to learn our way in the streets of Athens, and to know the tyranny of Aristophanes, requiring more genius and sometimes not less cruelty than belonged to the official commanders. Aristophanes is now very accessible, with much valuable commentary, through the labors of Mitchell and Cartwright. An excellent popular book is J. A. St. John's "Ancient Greece;" the "Life and Letters" of Niebuhr, even more than his Lectures, furnish leading views; and Winckelmann, a Greek born out of due time, has become essential to an intimate knowledge of the Attic genius. The secret of the recent histories in German and in English is the discovery, owed first to Wolff and later to Boeckh, that the sincere Greek history of that period must be drawn from Demosthenes, especially from the business orations; and from the comic poets.

If we come down a little by natural steps from the master to the disciples, we have, six or seven centuries later, the Platonists, who also cannot be skipped, — Plotinus, Porphyry, Proclus, Synesius, Jamblichus. Of Jamblichus the Emperor Julian said that "he was posterior to Plato in time, not in genius." Of Plotinus, we have eulogies by Porphyry and Longinus, and the favor of the Emperor Gallienus, indicating the respect he inspired among his contemporaries. If any one who had read with interest the "Isis and Osiris" of Plutarch should then read a chapter called "Providence," by Synesius, translated into English by Thomas Taylor, he will find it one of the majestic remains of literature, and, like one walking in the noblest of tem-

ples, will conceive new gratitude to his fellow-men,
and a new estimate of their nobility. The imaginative scholar will find few stimulants to his brain
like these writers. He has entered the Elysian
Fields ; and the grand and pleasing figures of gods
and dæmons and dæmoniacal men, of the "azonic"
and the "aquatic gods," dæmons with fulgid eyes,
and all the rest of the Platonic rhetoric, exalted a
little under the African sun, sail before his eyes.
The acolyte has mounted the tripod over the cave
at Delphi ; his heart dances, his sight is quickened.
These guides speak of the gods with such depth
and with such pictorial details, as if they had been
bodily present at the Olympian feasts. The reader
of these books makes new acquaintance with his
own mind ; new regions of thought are opened.
Jamblichus's "Life of Pythagoras" works more
directly on the will than the others; since Pythagoras was eminently a practical person, the founder
of a school of ascetics and socialists, a planter of
colonies, and nowise a man of abstract studies
alone.

The respectable and sometimes excellent translations of Bohn's Library have done for literature
what railroads have done for internal intercourse.
I do not hesitate to read all the books I have
named, and all good books, in translations. What
is really best in any book is translatable, — any

real insight or broad human sentiment. Nay, I observe that, in our Bible, and other books of lofty moral tone, it seems easy and inevitable to render the rhythm and music of the original into phrases of equal melody. The Italians have a fling at translators, — *i traditori traduttori ;* but I thank them. I rarely read any Latin, Greek, German, Italian, sometimes not a French book, in the original, which I can procure in a good version. I like to be beholden to the great metropolitan English speech, the sea which receives tributaries from every region under heaven. I should as soon think of swimming across Charles River when I wish to go to Boston, as of reading all my books in originals when I have them rendered for me in my mother-tongue.

For history there is great choice of ways to bring the student through early Rome. If he can read Livy, he has a good book; but one of the short English compends, some Goldsmith or Ferguson, should be used, that will place in the cycle the bright stars of Plutarch. The poet Horace is the eye of the Augustan age; Tacitus, the wisest of historians; and Martial will give him Roman manners, — and some very bad ones, — in the early days of the Empire: but Martial must be read, if read at all, in his own tongue. These will bring him to Gibbon, who will take him in charge and convey him with abundant entertainment down — with notice of all remarkable objects on the way — through fourteen hundred years of time. He cannot spare Gibbon, with his vast reading, with such wit and continuity of mind, that, though never profound, his book is one of the conveniences of civilization, like the new railroad from ocean to ocean, — and, I think, will be sure to send the reader to his "Memoirs of Himself," and the "Extracts from my Journal," and "Abstracts of my Readings," which will spur the laziest scholar to emulation of his prodigious performance.

Now having our idler safe down as far as the fall of Constantinople in 1453, he is in very good courses; for here are trusty hands waiting for him. The cardinal facts of European history are soon learned. There is Dante's poem, to open the Italian Republics of the Middle Age; Dante's "Vita Nuova," to explain Dante and Beatrice; and Boccaccio's "Life of Dante," a great man to describe a greater. To help us, perhaps a volume or two of M. Sismondi's "Italian Republics" will be as good as the entire sixteen. When we come to Michael Angelo, his Sonnets and Letters must be read, with his Life by Vasari, or, in our day, by Herman Grimm. For the Church and the Feudal Institution, Mr. Hallam's "Middle Ages" will furnish, if superficial, yet readable and conceivable outlines.

The " Life of the Emperor Charles V.," by the useful Robertson, is still the key of the following age. Ximenes, Columbus, Loyola, Luther, Erasmus, Melanchthon, Francis I., Henry VIII., Elizabeth, and Henry IV. of France, are his contemporaries. It is a time of seeds and expansions, whereof our recent civilization is the fruit.

If now the relations of England to European affairs bring him to British ground, he is arrived at the very moment when modern history takes new proportions. He can look back for the legends and mythology to the " Younger Edda " and the " Heimskringla " of Snorro Sturleson, to Mallet's " Northern Antiquities," to Ellis's " Metrical Romances," to Asser's " Life of Alfred " and Venerable Bede, and to the researches of Sharon Turner and Palgrave. Hume will serve him for an intelligent guide, and in the Elizabethan era he is at the richest period of the English mind, with the chief men of action and of thought which that nation has produced, and with a pregnant future before him. Here he has Shakspeare, Spenser, Sidney, Raleigh, Bacon, Chapman, Jonson, Ford, Beaumont and Fletcher, Herbert, Donne, Herrick ; and Milton, Marvell, and Dryden, not long after.

In reading history, he is to prefer the history of individuals. He will not repent the time he gives to Bacon, — not if he read the " Advancement of

Learning," the " Essays," the " Novum Organum,"
the " History of Henry VII.," and then all the
" Letters " (especially those to the Earl of Devonshire, explaining the Essex business), and all but
his " Apophthegms."

The task is aided by the strong mutual light
which these men shed on each other. Thus, the
works of Ben Jonson are a sort of hoop to bind all
these fine persons together, and to the land to which
they belong. He has written verses to or on all
his notable contemporaries; and what with so many
occasional poems, and the portrait sketches in his
" Discoveries," and the gossiping record of his
opinions in his conversations with Drummond of
Hawthornden, he has really illustrated the England
of his time, if not to the same extent yet much in
the same way, as Walter Scott has celebrated the
persons and places of Scotland. Walton, Chapman, Herrick, and Sir Henry Wotton write also
to the times.

Among the best books are certain *Autobiographies;* as, St. Augustine's Confessions; Benvenuto
Cellini's Life; Montaigne's Essays; Lord Herbert
of Cherbury's Memoirs; Memoirs of the Cardinal
de Retz; Rousseau's Confessions; Linnæus's Diary; Gibbon's, Hume's, Franklin's, Burns's, Al-
fieri's, Goethe's, and Haydon's Autobiographies.

Another class of books closely allied to these, and

of like interest, are those which may be called
Table-Talks: of which the best are Saadi's Gulistan; Luther's Table-Talk; Aubrey's Lives;
Spence's anecdotes; Selden's Table-Talk; Boswell's Life of Johnson; Eckermann's Conversations with Goethe; Coleridge's Table-Talk; and
Hazlitt's Life of Northcote.

There is a class whose value I should designate
as *Favorites:* such as Froissart's Chronicles;
Southey's Chronicle of the Cid; Cervantes; Sul-
ly's Memoirs; Rabelais; Montaigne; Izaak Walton; Evelyn; Sir Thomas Browne; Aubrey;
Sterne; Horace Walpole; Lord Clarendon; Doctor
Johnson; Burke, shedding floods of light on his
times; Lamb; Landor; and De Quincey; — a list,
of course, that may easily be swelled, as dependent
on individual caprice. Many men are as tender
·and irritable as lovers in reference to these predilec-
tions. Indeed, a man's library is a sort of harem,
and I observe that tender readers have a great pu-
dency in showing their books to a stranger.

The annals of bibliography afford many examples
of the delirious extent to which book-fancying can
go, when the legitimate delight in a book is trans-
ferred to a rare edition or to a manuscript. This
mania reached its height about the beginning of the
present century. For an autograph of Shakspeare
one hundred and fifty-five guineas were given. In

May, 1812, the library of the Duke of Roxburgh
was sold. The sale la. l forty-two days, — we
abridge the story from Dibdin, — and among the
many curiosities was a copy of Boccaccio published
by Valdarfer, at Venice, in 1471; the only perfect
copy of this edition. Among the distinguished
company which attended the sale were the Duke
of Devonshire, Earl Spencer, and the Duke of
Marlborough, then Marquis of Blandford. The
bid stood at five hundred guineas. " A thousand
guineas," said Earl Spencer: "And ten," added
the Marquis. You might hear a pin drop. All eyes
were bent on the bidders. Now they talked apart,
now ate a biscuit, now made a bet, but without the
least thought of yielding one to the other. But
to pass over some details, — the contest proceeded
until the Marquis said, " Two thousand pounds."
Earl Spencer bethought him like a prudent general
of useless bloodshed and waste of powder, and had
paused a quarter of a minute, when Lord Althorp
with long steps came to his side, as if to bring his
father a fresh lance to renew the fight. Father
and son whispered together, and Earl Spencer ex-
claimed, " Two thousand two hundred and fifty
pounds!" An electric shock went through the
assembly. "And ten," quietly added the Marquis.
There ended the strife. Ere Evans let the hammer
fall, he paused; the ivory instrument swept the

air ; the spectators stood dumb, when the hammer
fell. The stroke of its fall sounded on the farthest
shores of Italy. The tap of that hammer was
heard in the libraries of Rome, Milan, and Venice.
Boccaccio stirred in his sleep of five hundred years,
and M. Van Praet groped in vain among the royal
alcoves in Paris, to detect a copy of the famed Valdarfer Boccaccio.

Another class I distinguish by the term *Vocabu-
laries.* Burton's " Anatomy of Melancholy " is a
book of great learning. To read it is like reading
in a dictionary. 'T is an inventory to remind us
how many classes and species of facts exist, and,
in observing into what strange and multiplex by-
ways learning has strayed, to infer our opulence.
Neither is a dictionary a bad book to read. There
is no cant in it, no excess of explanation, and it is
full of suggestion, — the raw material of possible
poems and histories. Nothing is wanting but a little shuffling, sorting, ligature, and cartilage. Out
of a hundred examples, Cornelius Agrippa " On the
Vanity of Arts and Sciences " is a specimen of that
scribatiousness which grew to be the habit of the
gluttonous readers of his time. Like the modern
Germans, they read a literature while other mortals
read a few books. They read voraciously, and must
disburden themselves ; so they take any general
topic, as Melancholy, or Praise of Science, or Praise

of Folly, and write and quote without method or
end. Now and then out of that affluence of their
learning comes a fine sentence from Theophrastus,
or Seneca, or Boëthius, but no high method, no inspiring efflux. But one cannot afford to read for a
few sentences; they are good only as strings of sug-
gestive words.

There is another class, more needful to the present age, because the currents of custom run now in
another direction and leave us dry on this side;
— I mean the *Imaginative.* A right metaphysics
should do justice to the co-ordinate powers of Imagination, Insight, Understanding, and Will. Poetry,
with its aids of Mythology and Romance, must be
well allowed for an imaginative creature. Men
are ever lapsing into a beggarly habit, wherein
everything that is not ciphering, that is, which does
not serve the tyrannical animal, is hustled out of
sight. Our orators and writers are of the same
poverty, and in this rag-fair neither the Imagination, the great awakening power, nor the Morals,
creative of genius and of men, are addressed. But
though orator and poet be of this hunger party,
the capacities remain. We must have symbols.
The child asks you for a story, and is thankful for
the poorest. It is not poor to him, but radiant with
meaning. The man asks for a novel, — that is,
asks leave for a few hours to be a poet, and to

paint things as they ought to be. The youth asks
for a poem. The very dunces wish to go to the
theatre. What private heavens can we not open,
by yielding to all the suggestion of rich music! We
must have idolatries, mythologies, — some swing
and verge for the creative power lying coiled and
cramped here, driving ardent natures to insanity
and crime if it do not find vent. Without the
great arts which speak to the sense of beauty, a
man seems to me a poor, naked, shivering creature. These are his becoming draperies, which
warm and adorn him. Whilst the prudential and
economical tone of society starves the imagination,
affronted Nature gets such indemnity as she may.
The novel is that allowance and frolic the imagination finds. Everything else pins it down, and men
flee for redress to Byron, Scott, Disraeli, Dumas,
Sand, Balzac, Dickens, Thackeray, and Reade.
Their education is neglected; but the circulating-
library and the theatre, as well as the trout-fishing,
the Notch Mountains, the Adirondack country, the
tour to Mont Blanc, to the White Hills and the
Ghauts, make such amends as they can.

The imagination infuses a certain volatility and
intoxication. It has a flute which sets the atoms
of our frame in a dance, like planets; and once so
liberated, the whole man reeling drunk to the music, they never quite subside to their old stony state.

But what is the imagination? Only an arm or weapon of the interior energy : only the precursor of the reason. And books that treat the old pedantries of the world, our times, places, professions, customs, opinions, histories, with a certain freedom, and distribute things, not after the usages of America and Europe but after the laws of right reason, and with as daring a freedom as we use in dreams, put us on our feet again, enable us to form an original judgment of our duties, and suggest new thoughts for to-morrow.

"Lucrezia Floriani," "Le Péché de M. Antoine," "Jeanne," and "Consuelo," of George Sand, are great steps from the novel of one termination, which we all read twenty years ago. Yet how far off from life and manners and motives the novel still is! Life lies about us dumb ; the day, as we know it, has not yet found a tongue. These stories are to the plots of real life what the figures in "La Belle Assemblée," which represent the fashion of the month, are to portraits. But the novel will find the way to our interiors one day, and will not always be the novel of costume merely. I do not think it inoperative now. So much novel-reading cannot leave the young men and maidens untouched ; and doubtless it gives some ideal dignity to the day. The young study noble behavior ; and as the player in "Consuelo" insists that he and his

colleagues on the boards have taught princes the
fine etiquette and strokes of grace and dignity which
they practise with so much effect in their villas
and among their dependents, so I often see traces
of the Scotch or the French novel in the courtesy
and brilliancy of young midshipmen, collegians,
and clerks. Indeed, when one observes how ill and
ugly people make their loves and quarrels, 't is pity
they should not read novels a little more, to import
the fine generosities and the clear, firm conduct,
which are as becoming in the unions and separations which love effects under shingle roofs as in
palaces and among illustrious personages.

In novels the most serious questions are beginning to be discussed. What made the popularity
of "Jane Eyre," but that a central question was
answered in some sort? The question there answered in regard to a vicious marriage will always
be treated according to the habit of the party. A
person of commanding individualism will answer
it as Rochester does, — as Cleopatra, as Milton, as
George Sand do, — magnifying the exception into
a rule, dwarfing the world into an exception. A
person of less courage, that is of less constitution,
will answer as the heroine does, — giving way to
fate, to conventionalism, to the actual state and
doings of men and women.

For the most part, our novel-reading is a passion

for results. We admire parks, and high-born beauties, and the homage of drawing-rooms and parliaments. They make us skeptical, by giving prominence to wealth and social position.

I remember when some peering eyes of boys discovered that the oranges hanging on the boughs of an orange-tree in a gay piazza were tied to the twigs by thread. I fear 't is so with the novelist's prosperities. Nature has a magic by which she fits the man to his fortunes, by making them the fruit of his character. But the novelist plucks this event here and that fortune there, and ties them rashly to his figures, to tickle the fancy of his readers with a cloying success or scare them with shocks of tragedy. And so, on the whole, 't is a juggle. We are cheated into laughter or wonder by feats which only oddly combine acts that we do every day. There is no new element, no power, no furtherance. 'T is only confectionery, not the raising of new corn. Great is the poverty of their inventions. *She was beautiful and he fell in love.* Money, and killing, and the Wandering Jew, and persuading the lover that his mistress is betrothed to another, these are the main-springs; new names, but no new qualities in the men and women. Hence the vain endeavor to keep any bit of this fairy gold which has rolled like a brook through our hands. A thousand thoughts awoke; great rainbows seemed to span the sky, a morning among the mountains; but we close the book and not a ray remains in the memory of evening. But this passion for romance, and this disappointment, show how much we need real elevations and pure poetry: that which shall show us, in morning and night, in stars and mountains and in all the plight and circumstance of men, the analogons of our own thoughts, and a like impression made by a just book and by the face of Nature.

If our times are sterile in genius, we must cheer us with books of rich and believing men who had atmosphere and amplitude about them. Every good fable, every mythology, every biography from a religious age, every passage of love, and even philosophy and science, when they proceed from an intellectual integrity and are not detached and critical, have the imaginative element. The Greek fables, the Persian history (Firdusi), the "Younger Edda" of the Scandinavians, the "Chronicle of the Cid," the poem of Dante, the Sonnets of Michel Angelo, the English drama of Shakspeare, Beaumont and Fletcher, and Ford, and even the prose of Bacon and Milton, — in our time the Ode of Wordsworth, and the poems and the prose of Goethe, have this enlargement, and inspire hope and generous attempts.

There is no room left, — and yet I might as well

not have begun as to leave out a class of books
which are the best : I mean the Bibles of the world,
or the sacred books of each nation, which express
for each the supreme result of their experience.
After the Hebrew and Greek Scriptures, which
constitute the sacred books of Christendom, these
are, the Desatir of the Persians, and the Zoroas-
trian Oracles ; the Vedas and Laws of Menu ;
the Upanishads, the Vishnu Purana, the Bhagvat
Geeta, of the Hindoos ; the books of the Buddhists ;
the " Chinese Classic," of four books, containing
the wisdom of Confucius and Mencius.   Also such
other books as have acquired a semi-canonical au-
thority in the world, as expressing the highest sentiment and hope of nations.   Such are the " Her-
mes Trismegistus," pretending to be Egyptian remains ; the " Sentences " of Epictetus ; of Marcus
Antoninus ; the " Vishnu Sarma " of the Hindoos ;
the " Gulistan " of Saadi ; the " Imitation of Christ,"
of Thomas à Kempis ; and the " Thoughts " of
Pascal.

All these books are the majestic expressions of
the universal conscience, and are more to our daily
purpose than this year's almanac or this day's newspaper.   But they are for the closet, and to be read
on the bended knee.   Their communications are
not to be given or taken with the lips and the end
of the tongue, but out of the glow of the cheek, and

with the throbbing heart. Friendship should give
and take, solitude and time brood and ripen, heroes
absorb and enact them. They are not to be held
by letters printed on a page, but are living characters translatable into every tongue and form of life.
I read them on lichens and bark; I watch them on
waves on the beach; they fly in birds, they creep
in worms; I detect them in laughter and blushes
and eye-sparkles of men and women. These are
Scriptures which the missionary might well carry
over prairie, desert, and ocean, to Siberia, Japan,
Timbuctoo. Yet he will find that the spirit which
is in them journeys faster than he, and greets him
on his arrival, — was there already long before him.
The missionary must be carried by it, and find it
there, or he goes in vain. Is there any geography
in these things? We call them Asiatic, we call
them primeval; but perhaps that is only optical, for
Nature is always equal to herself, and there are as
good eyes and ears now in the planet as ever were.
Only these ejaculations of the soul are uttered one
or a few at a time, at long intervals, and it takes
millenniums to make a Bible.

These are a few of the books which the old and
the later times have yielded us, which will reward
the time spent on them. In comparing the number of good books with the shortness of life, many
might well be read by proxy, if we had good

proxies; and it would be well for sincere young men to borrow a hint from the French Institute and the British Association, and as they divide the whole body into sections, each of which sits upon and reports of certain matters confided to it, so let each scholar associate himself to such persons as he can rely on, in a literary club, in which each shall undertake a single work or series for which he is qualified. For example, how attractive is the whole literature of the " Roman de la Rose," the " Fabliaux," and the *gaie science* of the French Troubadours! Yet who in Boston has time for that? But one of our company shall undertake it, shall study and master it, and shall report on it as un ler oath; shall give us the sincere result as it lies in his mind, adding nothing, keeping nothing back. Another member meantime shall as honestly search, sift, and as truly report, on British mythology, the Round Table, the histories of Brut, Merlin, and Welsh poetry; a third on the Saxon Chronicles, Robert of Gloucester, and William of Malmesbury; a fourth, on Mysteries, Early Drama, " Gesta Romanorum," Collier, and Dyce, and the Camden Society. Each shall give us his grains of gold, after the washing; and every other shall then decide whether this is a book indispensable to him also.

CLUBS.

CLUBS.

WE are delicate machines, and require nice treatment to get from us the maximum of power and pleasure. We need tonics, but must have those that cost little or no reaction. The flame of life burns too fast in pure oxygen, and nature has tempered the air with nitrogen. So thought is the native air of the mind, yet pure it is a poison to our mixed constitution, and soon burns up the bonehouse of man, unless tempered with affection and coarse practice in the material world. Varied foods, climates, beautiful objects, — and especially the alternation of a large variety of objects, — are the necessity of this exigent system of ours. But our tonics, our luxuries, are force-pumps which exhaust the strength they pretend to supply; and of all the cordials known to us, the best, safest, and most exhilarating, with the least harm, is society; and every healthy and efficient mind passes a large part of life in the company most easy to him.

We seek society with very different aims, and the staple of conversation is widely unlike in its circles. Sometimes it is facts, — running from those of daily necessity, to the last results of science, — and has all degrees of importance; sometimes it is love, and makes the balm of our early and of our latest days; sometimes it is thought, as from a person who is a mind only; sometimes a singing, as if the heart poured out all like a bird; sometimes experience. With some men it is a debate; at the approach of a dispute they neigh like horses. Unless there be an argument, they think nothing is doing. Some talkers excel in the precision with which they formulate their thoughts, so that you get from them somewhat to remember; others lay criticism asleep by a charm. Especially women use words that are not words, — as steps in a dance are not steps, — but reproduce the genius of that they speak of; as the sound of some bells makes us think of the bell merely, whilst the church-chimes in the distance bring the church and its serious memories before us. Opinions are accidental in people, — have a poverty-stricken air. A man valuing himself as the organ of this or that dogma is a dull companion enough; but opinion native to the speaker is sweet and refreshing, and inseparable from his image. Neither do we by any means always go to people for conversation. How often to say nothing, — and yet must go; as a child will long for his companions, but among them plays by himself. 'T is only presence which we want. But one thing is certain, — at some rate, intercourse we must have. The experience of retired men is positive, — that we lose our days and are barren of thought for want of some person to talk with. The · understanding can no more empty itself by its own action than can a deal box.

The clergyman walks from house to house all day all the year to give people the comfort of good talk. The physician helps them mainly in the same way, by healthy talk giving a right tone to the patient's mind. The dinner, the walk, the fireside, all have that for their main end.

See how Nature has secured the communication of knowledge. 'T is certain that money does not more burn in a boy's pocket than a piece of news burns in our memory until we can tell it. And in higher activity of mind, every new perception is attended with a thrill of pleasure, and the imparting of it to others is also attended with pleasure. Thought is the child of the intellect, and this child is conceived with joy and born with joy.

Conversation is the laboratory and workshop of the student. The affection or sympathy helps. The wish to speak to the want of another mind assists to clear your own. A certain truth possesses us which we in all ways strive to utter. Every time we say a thing in conversation, we get a mechanical advantage in detaching it well and deliverly. I prize the mechanics of conversation. 'T is pulley and lever and screw. To fairly disengage the mass, and send it jingling down, a good boulder, — a block of quartz and gold, to be worked up at leisure in the useful arts of life, — is a wonderful relief.

What are the best days in memory? Those in which we met a companion who was truly such. How sweet those hours when the day was not long enough to communicate and compare our intellectual jewels, — the favorite passages of each book, the proud anecdotes of our heroes, the delicious verses we had hoarded! What a motive had then our solitary days! How the countenance of our friend still left some light after he had gone! We remember the time when the best gift we could ask of fortune was to fall in with a valuable companion in a ship's cabin, or on a long journey in the old stage-coach, where, each passenger being forced to know every other, and other employments being out of question, conversation naturally flowed, people became rapidly acquainted, and, if well adapted, more intimate in a day than if they had been neighbors for years.

In youth, in the fury of curiosity and acquisition, the day is too short for books and the crowd of thoughts, and we are impatient of interruption.

Later, when books tire, thought has a more languid flow; and the days come when we are alarmed, and say there are no thoughts. 'What a barren-witted pate is mine!' the student says; 'I will go and learn whether I have lost my reason.' He seeks intelligent persons, whether more wise or less wise than he, who give him provocation, and at once and easily the old motion begins in his brain: thoughts, fancies, humors flow; the cloud lifts; the horizon broadens; and the infinite opulence of things is again shown him. But the right conditions must be observed. Mainly he must have leave to be himself. Sancho Panza blessed the man who invented sleep. So I prize the good invention whereby everybody is provided with somebody who is glad to see him.

If men are less when together than they are alone, they are also in some respects enlarged. They kindle each other; and such is the power of suggestion that each sprightly story calls out more; and sometimes a fact that had long slept in the recesses of memory hears the voice, is welcomed to daylight, and proves of rare value. Every metaphysician must have observed, not only that no thought is alone, but that thoughts commonly go in pairs; though the related thoughts first appeared in his mind at long distances of time. Things are in pairs: a natural fact has only half its value until

a fact in moral nature, its counterpart, is stated.
Then they confirm and adorn each other; a story
is matched by another story. And that may be
the reason why, when a gentleman has told a good
thing, he immediately tells it again.

Nothing seems so cheap as the benefit of conversation; nothing is more rare. 'T is wonderful how
you are balked and baffled. There is plenty of intelligence, reading, curiosity; but serious, happy
discourse, avoiding personalities, dealing with results, is rare: and I seldom meet with a reading
and thoughtful person but he tells me, as if it were
his exceptional mishap, that he has no companion.

Suppose such a one to go out exploring different
circles in search of this wise and genial counterpart, — he might inquire far and wide. Conversation in society is found to be on a platform so low
as to exclude science, the saint, and the poet.
Amidst all the gay banter, sentiment cannot profane itself and venture out. The reply of old Isocrates comes so often to mind, — "The things which
are now seasonable I cannot say; and for the things
which I can say it is not now the time." Besides,
who can resist the charm of talent? The lover of
letters loves power too. Among the men of wit
and learning, he could not withhold his homage
from the gayety, grasp of memory, luck, splendor,
and speed; such exploits of discourse, such feats of

society! What new powers, what mines of wealth! But when he came home, his brave sequins were dry leaves. He found either that the fact they had thus dizened and adorned was of no value, or that he already knew all and more than all they had told him. He could not find that he was helped by so much as one thought or principle, one solid fact, one commanding impulse: great was the dazzle, but the gain was small. He uses his occasions; he seeks the company of those who have convivial talent. But the moment they meet, to be sure they begin to be something else than they were; they play pranks, dance jigs, run on each other, pun, tell stories, try many fantastic tricks, under some superstition that there must be excitement and elevation; — and they kill conversation at once. I know well the rusticity of the shy hermit. No doubt he does not make allowance enough for men of more active blood and habit. But it is only on natural ground that conversation can be rich. It must not begin with uproar and violence. Let it keep the ground, let it feel the connection with the battery. Men must not be off their centres.

Some men love only to talk where they are masters. They like to go to school-girls, or to boys, or into the shops where the sauntering people gladly lend an ear to any one. On these terms they give information and please themselves by sallies and chat which are admired by the idlers; and the talker is at his ease and jolly, for he can walk out without ceremony when he pleases. They go rarely to their equals, and then as for their own convenience simply, making too much haste to introduce and impart their new whim or discovery; listen badly or do not listen to the comment or to the thought by which the company strive to repay them; rather, as soon as their own speech is done, they take their hats. Then there are the gladiators, to whom it is always a battle; 'tis no matter on which side, they fight for victory; then the heady men, the egotists, the monotones, the steriles, and the impracticables.

It does not help that you find as good or a better man than yourself, if he is not timed and fitted to you. The greatest sufferers are often those who have the most to say, — men of a delicate sympathy, who are dumb in mixed company. Able people, if they do not know how to make allowance for them, paralyze them. One of those conceited prigs who value nature only as it feeds and exhibits them is equally a pest with the roysterers. There must be large reception as well as giving. How delightful after these disturbers is the radiant, playful wit of — one whom I need not name, — for in every society there is his representative. Good-nature is stronger than tomahawks. His conversation is all pictures: he can reproduce whatever he has seen; he tells the best story in the county, and is of such genial temper that he disposes all others irresistibly to good-humor and discourse. Diderot said of the Abbé Galiani: "He was a treasure in rainy days; and if the cabinet-makers made such things, everybody would have one in the country."

One lesson we learn early, — that in spite of seeming difference, men are all of one pattern. We readily assume this with our mates, and are disappointed and angry if we find that we are premature, and that their watches are slower than ours. In fact the only sin which we never forgive in each other is difference of opinion. We know beforehand that yonder man must think as we do. Has he not two hands, — two feet, — hair and nails? Does he not eat, — bleed, — laugh, — cry? His dissent from me is the veriest affectation. This conclusion is at once the logic of persecution and of love. And the ground of our indignation is our conviction that his dissent is some wilfulness he practises on himself. He checks the flow of his opinion, as the cross cow holds up her milk. Yes, and we look into his eye, and see that he knows it and hides his eye from ours.

But to come a little nearer to my mark, I am to say that there may easily be obstacles in the way of finding the pure article we are in search of, but when we find it it is worth the pursuit, for beside its comfort as medicine and cordial, once in the right company, new and vast values do not fail to appear. All that man can do for man is to be found in that market. There are great prizes in this game. Our fortunes in the world are as our mental equipment for this competition is. Yonder is a man who can answer the questions which I cannot. Is it so? Hence comes to me boundless curiosity to know his experiences and his wit. Hence competition for the stakes dearest to man. What is a match at whist, or draughts, or billiards, or chess, to a match of mother-wit, of knowledge, and of resources? However courteously we conceal it, it is social rank and spiritual power that are compared; whether in the parlor, the courts, the caucus, the senate, or the chamber of science, — which are only less or larger theatres for this competition.

He that can define, he that can answer a question so as to admit of no further answer, is the best man. This was the meaning of the story of the Sphinx. In the old time conundrums were sent from king to king by ambassadors. The seven wise masters at Periander's banquet spent their time in answering them. The life of Socrates is a propounding and a solution of these. So, in the hagiology of each nation, the lawgiver was in each case some man of eloquent tongue, whose sympathy brought him face to face with the extremes of society. Jesus, Menu, the first Buddhist, Mahomet, Zertusht, Pythagoras, are examples.

Jesus spent his life in discoursing with humble people on life and duty, in giving wise answers, showing that he saw at a larger angle of vision, and at least silencing those who were not generous enough to accept his thoughts. Luther spent his life so; and it is not his theologic works, — his " Commentary on the Galatians," and the rest, but his " Table-Talk," which is still read by men. Dr. Johnson was a man of no profound mind, — full of English limitations, English politics, English Church, Oxford philosophy; yet, having a large heart, mother-wit, and good sense which impatiently overleaped his customary bounds, his conversation as reported by Boswell has a lasting charm. Conversation is the vent of character as well as of thought; and Dr. Johnson impresses his company, not only by the point of the remark, but also, when the point fails, because *he* makes it. His obvious religion or superstition, his deep wish that they should think so or so, weighs with them, — so rare is depth of feeling, or a constitutional value for a thought or opinion, among the light-minded men and women who make up society; and though they know that there is in the speaker a degree of short-coming, of insincerity, and of talking for victory, yet the existence of character, and habitual reverence for principles over talent or learning, is felt by the frivolous.

One of the best records of the great German master who towered over all his contemporaries in the first thirty years of this century, is his conversations as recorded by Eckermann ; and the "Table-Talk" of Coleridge is one of the best remains of his genius.

In the Norse legends, the gods of Valhalla, when they meet the Jotuns, converse on the perilous terms that he who cannot answer the other's questions forfeits his own life. Odin comes to the threshold of the Jotun Wafthrudnir in disguise, calling himself Gangrader; is invited into the hall, and told that he cannot go out thence unless he can answer every question Wafthrudnir shall put. Wafthrudnir asks him the name of the god of the sun, and of the god who brings the night; what river separates the dwellings of the sons of the giants from those of the gods; what plain lies between the gods and Surtur, their adversary, etc. ; all which the disguised Odin answers satisfactorily. Then it is his turn to interrogate, and he is answered well for a time by the Jotun. At last he puts a question which none but himself could answer: " What did Odin whisper in the ear of his son Balder, when Balder mounted the funeral pile ? " The startled giant replies : " None of the gods knows what in the old time THOU saidst in the ear of thy son : with death on my mouth have I spoken the fate-words of the generation of the Æsir ; with Odin contended I in wise words. Thou must ever the wisest be."

And still the gods and giants are so known, and still they play the same game in all the million mansions of heaven and of earth ; at all tables, clubs, and *tête-à-têtes*, the lawyers in the court-house, the senators in the capitol, the doctors in the academy, the wits in the hotel. Best is he who gives an answer that cannot be answered again. *Omnis definitio periculosa est,* and only wit has the secret. The same thing took place when Leibnitz came to visit Newton ; when Schiller came to Goethe ; when France, in the person of Madame de Staël visited Goethe and Schiller ; when Hegel was the guest of Victor Cousin in Paris ; when Linnæus was the guest of Jussieu. It happened many years ago that an American chemist carried a letter of introduction to Dr. Dalton of Manchester, England, the author of the theory of atomic proportions, and was coolly enough received by the Doctor in the laboratory where he was engaged. Only Dr. Dalton scratched a formula on a scrap

of paper and pushed it towards the guest, — "Had
he seen that?" The visitor scratched on another
paper a formula describing some results of his own
with sulphuric acid, and pushed it across the table,
— "Had he seen that?" The attention of the
English chemist was instantly arrested, and they
became rapidly acquainted.

To answer a question so as to admit of no reply,
is the test of a man, — to touch bottom every time.
Hyde, Earl of Rochester, asked Lord-Keeper Guil-
ford, "Do you not think I could understand any
business in England in a month?" "Yes, my
lord," replied the other, "but I think you would
understand it better in two months." When Ed-
ward I. claimed to be acknowledged by the Scotch
(1292) as lord paramount, the nobles of Scotland
replied, "No answer can be made while the throne
is vacant." When Henry III. (1217) plead du-
ress against his people demanding confirmation and
execution of the Charter, the reply was: "If this
were admitted, civil wars could never close but by
the extirpation of one of the contending parties."

What can you do with one of these sharp respon-
dents? What can you do with an eloquent man?
No rules of debate, no contempt of court, no exclu-
sions, no gag-laws can be contrived that his first
syllable will not set aside or overstep and annul.
You can shut out the light, it may be, but can you

shut out gravitation? You may condemn his book, but can you fight against his thought? That is always too nimble for you, anticipates you, and breaks out victorious in some other quarter. Can you stop the motions of good sense? What can you do with Beaumarchais, who converts the censor whom the court has appointed to stifle his play into an ardent advocate? The court appoints another censor, who shall crush it this time. Beaumarchais persuades him to defend it. The court successively appoints three more severe inquisitors; Beaumarchais converts them all into triumphant vindicators of the play which is to bring in the Revolution. Who can stop the mouth of Luther, — of Newton? — of Franklin, — of Mirabeau, — of Talleyrand?

These masters can make good their own place, and need no patron. Every variety of gift — science, religion, politics, letters, art, prudence, war, or love — has its vent and exchange in conversation. Conversation is the Olympic games whither every superior gift resorts to assert and approve itself, — and, of course, the inspirations of powerful and public men, with the rest. But it is not this class, whom the splendor of their accomplishment almost inevitably guides into the vortex of ambition, makes them chancellors and commanders of council and of action, and makes them at last fatalists, — not these whom we now consider. We consider those who are interested in thoughts, their own and other men's, and who delight in comparing them; who think it the highest compliment they can pay a man to deal with him as an intellect, to expose to him the grand and cheerful secrets perhaps never opened to their daily companions, to share with him the sphere of freedom and the simplicity of truth.

But the best conversation is rare. Society seems to have agreed to treat fictions as realities, and realities as fictions; and the simple lover of truth, especially if on very high grounds, as a religious or intellectual seeker, finds himself a stranger and alien.

It is possible that the best conversation is between two persons who can talk only to each other. Even Montesquieu confessed that in conversation, if he perceived he was listened to by a third person, it seemed to him from that moment the whole question vanished from his mind. I have known persons of rare ability who were heavy company to good social men who knew well enough how to draw out others of retiring habit; and, moreover, were heavy to intellectual men who ought to have known them. And does it never occur that we perhaps live with people too superior to be seen, — as there are musical notes too high for the scale of most ears? There are men who are great only to one or two companions of more opportunity, or more adapted.

It was to meet these wants that in all civil nations attempts have been made to organize conversation by bringing together cultivated people under the most favorable conditions. 'Tis certain there was liberal and refined conversation in the Greek, in the Roman, and in the Middle Age. There was a time when in France a revolution occurred in domestic architecture; when the houses of the nobility, which, up to that time, had been constructed on feudal necessities, in a hollow square, — the ground-floor being resigned to offices and stables, and the floors above to rooms of state and to lodging-rooms, — were rebuilt with new purpose. It was the Marchioness of Rambouillet who first got the horses out of and the scholars into the palaces, having constructed her *hôtel* with a view to society, with superb suites of drawing-rooms on the same floor, and broke through the *morgue* of etiquette by inviting to her house men of wit and learning as well as men of rank, and piqued the emulation of Cardinal Richelieu to rival assemblies, and so to the founding of the French Academy. The history of the Hôtel Rambouillet and its brilliant circles makes an important date in French civilization. And a history of clubs from early antiquity, tracing the efforts to secure liberal and refined con-

versation, through the Greek and Roman to the
Middle Age, and thence down through French,
English, and German memoirs, tracing the clubs
and coteries in each country, would be an important chapter in history. We know well the Mer-
maid Club, in London, of Shakspeare, Ben Jonson, Chapman, Herrick, Selden, Beaumont and
Fletcher; its " Rules " are preserved, and many
allusions to their suppers are found in Jonson,
Herrick, and in Aubrey. Anthony Wood has
many details of Harrington's Club. Dr. Bentley's
Club held Newton, Wren, Evelyn, and Locke; and
we owe to Boswell our knowledge of the club of
Dr. Johnson, Goldsmith, Burke, Gibbon, Reynolds,
Garrick, Beauclerk and Percy. And we have records of the brilliant society that Edinburgh boasted
in the first decade of this century. Such societies
are possible only in great cities, and are the compensation which these can make to their dwellers
for depriving them of the free intercourse with
Nature. Every scholar is surrounded by wiser
men than he — if they cannot write as well. Cannot they meet and exchange results to their mutual
benefit and delight? It was a pathetic experience
when a genial and accomplished person said to me,
looking from his country home to the capital of
New England, "There is a town of two hundred
thousand people, and not a chair in it for me." If

he were sure to find at No. 2000 Tremont Street what scholars were abroad after the morning studies were ended, Boston would shine as the New Jerusalem to his eyes.

Now this want of adapted society is mutual. The man of thought, the man of letters, the man of science, the administrator skilful in affairs, the man of manners and culture, whom you so much wish to find, — each of these is wishing to be found. Each wishes to open his thought, his knowledge, his social skill to the daylight in your company and affection, and to exchange his gifts for yours; and the first hint of a select and intelligent company is welcome.

But the club must be self-protecting, and obstacles arise at the outset. There are people who cannot well be cultivated; whom you must keep down and quiet if you can. There are those who have the instinct of a bat to fly against any lighted candle and put it out, — marplots and contradictors. There are those who go only to talk, and those who go only to hear: both are bad. A right rule for a club would be, — Admit no man whose presence excludes any one topic. It requires people who are not surprised and shocked, who do and let do and let be, who sink trifles and know solid values, and who take a great deal for granted.

It is always a practical difficulty with clubs to

regulate the laws of election so as to exclude peremptorily every social nuisance. Nobody wishes bad manners. We must have loyalty and character. The poet Marvell was wont to say that he "would not drink wine with any one with whom he could not trust his life." But neither can we afford to be superfine. A man of irreproachable behavior and excellent sense preferred on his travels taking his chance at a hotel for company, to the charging himself with too many select letters of introduction. He confessed he liked low company. He said the fact was incontestable that the society of gypsies was more attractive than that of bishops. The girl deserts the parlor for the kitchen; the boy, for the wharf. Tutors and parents cannot interest him like the uproarious conversation he finds in the market or the dock. I knew a scholar, of some experience in camps, who said that he liked, in a bar-room, to tell a few coon stories and put himself on a good footing with the company; then he could be as silent as he chose. A scholar does not wish to be always pumping his brains; he wants gossips. The black-coats are good company only for black-coats; but when the manufacturers, merchants, and shipmasters meet, see how much they have to say, and how long the conversation lasts! They have come from many zones; they have traversed wide countries; they know each his own arts, and the cunning

artisans of his craft; they have seen the best and
the worst of men. Their knowledge contradicts
the popular opinion and your own on many points.
Things which you fancy wrong they know to be
right and profitable; things which you reckon
superstitious they know to be true. They have
found virtue in the strangest homes; and in the
rich store of their adventures are instances and
examples which you have been seeking in vain for
years, and which they suddenly and unwittingly
offer you.

I remember a social experiment in this direction, wherein it appeared that each of the members
fancied he was in need of society, but himself un-
presentable. On trial they all found that they
could be tolerated by, and could tolerate, each
other. Nay, the tendency to extreme self-respect
which hesitated to join in a club was running rapidly down to abject admiration of each other, when
the club was broken up by new combinations.

The use of the hospitality of the club hardly
needs explanation. Men are unbent and social at
table; and I remember it was explained to me, in
a Southern city, that it was impossible to set any
public charity on foot unless through a tavern dinner. I do not think our metropolitan charities
would plead the same necessity; but to a club met
for conversation a supper is a good basis, as it dis-

arms all parties and puts pedantry and business to
the door. All are in good humor and at leisure,
which are the first conditions of discourse; the ordinary reserves are thrown off, experienced men
meet with the freedom of boys, and, sooner or later,
impart all that is singular in their experience.

The hospitalities of clubs are easily exaggerated.
No doubt the suppers of wits and philosophers acquire much lustre by time and renown. Plutarch,
Xenophon, and Plato, who have celebrated each a
banquet of their set, have given us next to no data
of the viands; and it is to be believed that an in-
different tavern dinner in such society was more
relished by the *convives* than a much better one in
worse company. Herrick's verses to Ben Jonson
no doubt paint the fact: —

> " When we such clusters had
>   As made us nobly wild, not mad;
>   And yet, each verse of thine
>   Outdid the meat, outdid the frolic wine."

Such friends make the feast satisfying; and I notice
that it was when things went prosperously, and the
company was full of honor, at the banquet of the
Cid, that " the guests all were joyful, and agreed
in one thing, — that they had not eaten better for
three years."

I need only hint the value of the club for bringing masters in their several arts to compare and ex-

pand their views, to come to an understanding on these points, and so that their united opinion shall have its just influence on public questions of education and politics. It is agreed that in the sections of the British Association more information is mutually and effectually communicated, in a few hours, than in many months of ordinary correspondence and the printing and transmission of ponderous reports. We know that *l'homme de lettres* is a little wary, and not fond of giving away his seed-corn; but there is an infallible way to draw him out, namely, by having as good as he. If you have Tuscaroora and he Canada, he may exchange kernel for kernel. If his discretion is incurable, and he dare not speak of fairy gold, he will yet tell what new books he has found, what old ones recovered, what men write and read abroad. A principal purpose also is the hospitality of the club, as a means of receiving a worthy foreigner with mutual advantage.

Every man brings into society some partial thought and local culture. We need range and alternation of topics and variety of minds. One likes in a companion a phlegm which it is a triumph to disturb, and, not less, to make in an old acquaintance unexpected discoveries of scope and power through the advantage of an inspiring subject. Wisdom is like electricity. There is no permanently wise man, but men capable of wisdom, who, being put into certain company, or other favorable conditions, become wise for a short time, as glasses rubbed acquire electric power for a while. But while we look complacently at these obvious pleasures and values of good companions, I do not forget that Nature is always very much in earnest, and that her great gifts have something serious and stern. When we look for the highest benefits of conversation, the Spartan rule of one to one is usually enforced. Discourse, when it rises highest and searches deepest, when it lifts us into that mood out of which thoughts come that remain as stars in our firmament, is between two.

COURAGE.

COURAGE.

I OBSERVE that there are three qualities which conspicuously attract the wonder and reverence of mankind : —

1. Disinterestedness, as shown in indifference to the ordinary bribes and influences of conduct, — a purpose so sincere and generous that it cannot be tempted aside by any prospects of wealth or other private advantage. Self-love is, in almost all men, such an over-weight, that they are incredulous of a man's habitual preference of the general good to his own; but when they see it proved by sacrifices of ease, wealth, rank, and of life itself, there is no limit to their admiration. This has made the power of the saints of the East and West, who have led the religion of great nations. Self-sacrifice is the real miracle out of which all the reported miracles grew. This makes the renown of the heroes of Greece and Rome, — of Socrates, Aristides, and Phocion; of Quintus Curtius, Cato, and Regulus; of Hatem Tai's hospitality; of Chatham, whose scornful magnanimity gave him immense

popularity; of Washington, giving his service to the public without salary or reward.

2. Practical power. Men admire the man who can organize their wishes and thoughts in stone and wood and steel and brass, — the man who can build the boat, who has the impiety to make the rivers run the way he wants them; who can lead his telegraph through the ocean from shore to shore; who, sitting in his closet, can lay out the plans of a campaign, sea-war and land-war, such that the best generals and admirals, when all is done, see that they must thank him for success; the power of better combination and foresight, however exhibited, whether it only plays a game of chess, or whether, more loftily, a cunning mathematician, penetrating the cubic weights of stars, predicts the planet which eyes had never seen; or whether, exploring the chemical elements whereof we and the world are made, and seeing their secret, Franklin draws off the lightning in his hand; suggesting that one day a wiser geology shall make the earthquake harmless and the volcano an agricultural resource. Or here is one who, seeing the wishes of men, knows how to come at their end; whispers to this friend, argues down that adversary, moulds society to his purpose, and looks at all men as wax for his hands; takes command of them as the wind does of clouds, as the mother does of the child, or the man that

knows more does of the man that knows less, and leads them in glad surprise to the very point where they would be: this man is followed with acclamation.

3. The third excellence is courage, the perfect will, which no terrors can shake, which is attracted by frowns or threats or hostile armies, nay, needs these to awake and fan its reserved energies into a pure flame, and is never quite itself until the hazard is extreme; then it is serene and fertile, and all its powers play well. There is a Hercules, an Achilles, a Rustem, an Arthur or a Cid in the mythology of every nation; and in authentic history, a Leonidas, a Scipio, a Cæsar, a Richard Cœur de Lion, a Cromwell, a Nelson, a Great Condé, a Bertrand du Guesclin, a Doge Dandolo, a Napoleon, a Massena, and Ney. 'T is said courage is common, but the immense esteem in which it is held proves it to be rare. Animal resistance, the instinct of the male animal when cornered, is no doubt common; but the pure article, courage with eyes, courage with conduct, self-possession at the cannon's mouth, cheerfulness in lonely adherence to the right, is the endowment of elevated characters. I need not show how much it is esteemed, for the people give it the first rank. They forgive everything to it. What an ado we make through two thousand years about Thermopylæ and Sala-

mis! What a memory of Poitiers and Crecy, and Bunker Hill, and Washington's endurance! And any man who puts his life in peril in a cause which is esteemed becomes the darling of all men. The very nursery-books, the ballads which delight boys, the romances which delight men, the favorite topics of eloquence, the thunderous emphasis which orators give to every martial defiance and passage of arms, and which the people greet, may testify. How short a time since this whole nation rose every morning to read or to hear the traits of courage of its sons and brothers in the field, and was never weary of the theme! We have had examples of men who, for showing effective courage on a single occasion, have become a favorite spectacle to nations, and must be brought in chariots to every mass meeting.

Men are so charmed with valor that they have pleased themselves with being called lions, leopards, eagles, and dragons, from the animals contemporary with us in the geologic formations. But the animals have great advantage of us in precocity. Touch the snapping-turtle with a stick, and he seizes it with his teeth. Cut off his head, and the teeth will not let go the stick. Break the egg of the young, and the little embryo, before yet the eyes are open, bites fiercely; these vivacious creatures contriving, — shall we say? — not only to bite after they are dead, but also to bite before they are born.

But man begins life helpless. The babe is in paroxysms of fear the moment its nurse leaves it alone, and it comes so slowly to any power of self-protection that mothers say the salvation of the life and health of a young child is a perpetual miracle. The terrors of the child are quite reasonable, and add to his loveliness; for his utter ignorance and weakness, and his enchanting indignation on such a small basis of capital compel every by-stander to take his part. Every moment as long as he is awake he studies the use of his eyes, ears, hands, and feet, learning how to meet and avoid his dangers, and thus every hour loses one terror more. But this education stops too soon. A large majority of men being bred in families and beginning early to be occupied day by day with some routine of safe industry, never come to the rough experiences that make the Indian, the soldier, or the frontiersman self-subsistent and fearless. Hence the high price of courage indicates the general timidity. "Mankind," said Franklin, "are dastardly when they meet with opposition." In war even generals are seldom found eager to give battle. Lord Wellington said, "Uniforms were often masks;" and again, "When my journal appears, many statues must come down." The Norse Sagas

relate that when Bishop Magne reproved King
Sigurd for his wicked divorce, the priest who attended the bishop, expecting every moment when
the savage king would burst with rage and slay his
superior, said that he " saw the sky no bigger than
a calf-skin." And I remember when a pair of
Irish girls who had been run away with in a wagon
by a skittish horse, said that when he began to
rear, they were so frightened that they could not
see the horse.

Cowardice shuts the eyes till the sky is not
larger than a calf-skin; shuts the eyes so that we
cannot see the horse that is running away with us;
worse, shuts the eyes of the mind and chills the
heart. Fear is cruel and mean. The political
reigns of terror have been reigns of madness and
malignity, — a total perversion of opinion; society
is upside down, and its best men are thought too
bad to live. Then the protection which a house, a
family, neighborhood and property, even the first
accumulation of savings gives, go in all times to
generate this taint of the respectable classes.
Those political parties which gather-in the well-dis-
posed portion of the community, — how infirm and
ignoble! what white lips they have! always on the
defensive, as if the lead were intrusted to the journals, often written in great part by women and
boys, who, without strength, wish to keep up the ap-

pearance of strength. They can do the hurras, the placarding, the flags, — and the voting, if it is a fair day; but the aggressive attitude of men who will have right done, will no longer be bothered with burglars and ruffians in the streets, counterfeiters in public offices, and thieves on the bench; that part, the part of the leader and soul of the vigilance committee, must be taken by stout and sincere men who are really angry and determined. In ordinary, we have a snappish criticism which watches and contradicts the opposite party. We want the will which advances and dictates. When we get an advantage, as in Congress the other day, it is because our adversary has committed a fault, not that we have taken the initiative and given the law. Nature has made up her mind that what cannot defend itself shall not be defended. Complaining never so loud and with never so much reason is of no use. One heard much cant of peace-parties long ago in Kansas and elsewhere, that their strength lay in the greatness of their wrongs, and dissuading all resistance, as if to make this strength greater. But were their wrongs greater than the negro's? And what kind of strength did they ever give him? It was always invitation to the tyrant, and bred disgust in those who would protect the victim. What cannot stand must fall; and the measure of our sincerity and therefore of the

respect of men, is the amount of health and wealth
we will hazard in the defence of our right. An
old farmer, my neighbor across the fence, when I
ask him if he is not going to town-meeting, says:
" No; 'tis no use balloting, for it will not stay; but
what you do with the gun will stay so." Nature
has charged every one with his own defence as with
his own support, and the only title I can have to
your help is when I have manfully put forth all the
means I possess to keep me, and being overborne
by odds, the by-standers have a natural wish to interfere and see fair play.

But with this pacific education we have no readiness for bad times. I am much mistaken if every
man who went to the army in the late war had not
a lively curiosity to know how he should behave in
action. Tender, amiable boys, who had never encountered any rougher play than a base-ball match
or a fishing excursion, were suddenly drawn up to
face a bayonet charge or capture a battery. Of
course they must each go into that action with a
certain despair. Each whispers to himself: " My
exertions must be of small account to the result;
only will the benignant Heaven save me from dis-
gracing myself and my friends and my State. Die!
O yes, I can well die; but I cannot afford to mis-
behave; and I do not know how I shall feel." So
great a soldier as the old French Marshal Montluc

acknowledges that he has often trembled with fear, and recovered courage when he had said a prayer for the occasion. I knew a young soldier who died in the early campaign, who confided to his sister that he had made up his mind to volunteer for the war. "I have not," he said, "any proper courage, but I shall never let any one find it out." And he had accustomed himself always to go into whatever place of danger, and do whatever he was afraid to do, setting a dogged resolution to resist this natural infirmity. Coleridge has preserved an anecdote of an officer in the British Navy who told him that when he, in his first boat expedition, a midshipman in his fourteenth year, accompanied Sir Alexander Ball, " as we were rowing up to the vessel we were to attack, amid a discharge of musketry, I was overpowered with fear, my knees shook and I was ready to faint away. Lieutenant Ball seeing me, placed himself close beside me, took hold of my hand and whispered, ' Courage, my dear boy! you will recover in a minute or so ; I was just the same when I first went out in this way.' It was as if an angel spoke to me. From that moment I was as fearless and as forward as the oldest of the boat's crew. But I dare not think what would have become of me, if, at that moment, he had scoffed and exposed me."

Knowledge is the antidote to fear, — Knowledge,

Use, and Reason, with its higher aids. The child
is as much in danger from a staircase, or the fire-
grate, or a bath-tub, or a cat, as the soldier from a
cannon or an ambush. Each surmounts the fear
as fast as he precisely understands the peril and
learns the means of resistance. Each is liable to
panic, which is, exactly, the terror of ignorance
surrendered to the imagination. Knowledge is the
encourager, knowledge that takes fear out of the
heart, knowledge and use, which is knowledge in
practice. They can conquer who believe they can.
It is he who has done the deed once who does not
shrink from attempting it again. It is the groom
who knows the jumping horse well who can safely
ride him. It is the veteran soldier, who, seeing the
flash of the cannon, can step aside from the path of
the ball. Use makes a better soldier than the most
urgent considerations of duty, — familiarity with
danger enabling him to estimate the danger. He
sees how much is the risk, and is not afflicted with
imagination; knows practically Marshal Saxe's rule,
that every soldier killed costs the enemy his weight
in lead.

The sailor loses fear as fast as he acquires command of sails and spars and steam; the frontiersman, when he has a perfect rifle and has acquired
a sure aim. To the sailor's experience every new
circumstance suggests what he must do. The ter-

rific chances which make the hours and the minutes
long to the passenger, he whiles away by incessant
application of expedients and repairs. To him a
leak, a hurricane, or a water-spout is so much work,
— no more. The hunter is not alarmed by bears,
catamounts, or wolves, nor the grazier by his bull,
nor the dog-breeder by his bloodhound, nor an Arab
by the simoon, nor a farmer by a fire in the woods.
The forest on fire looks discouraging enough to a
citizen : the farmer is skilful to fight it. The
neighbors run together ; with pine boughs they can
mop out the flame, and by raking with the hoe a
long but little trench, confine to a patch the fire
which would easily spread over a hundred acres.

In short, courage consists in equality to the problem before us. The school-boy is daunted before
his tutor by a question of arithmetic, because he
does not yet command the simple steps of the solution which the boy beside him has mastered. These
once seen, he is as cool as Archimedes, and cheerily
proceeds a step farther. Courage is equality to the
problem, in affairs, in science, in trade, in council,
or in action ; consists in the conviction that the
agents with whom you contend are not superior in
strength of resources or spirit to you. The general
must stimulate the mind of his soldiers to the perception that they are men, and the enemy is no
more. Knowledge, yes ; for the danger of dangers

is illusion. The eye is easily daunted; and the drums, flags, shining helmets, beard, and moustache of the soldier have conquered you long before his sword or bayonet reaches you.

But we do not exhaust the subject in the slight analysis; we must not forget the variety of temperaments, each of which qualifies this power of resistance. It is observed that men with little imagination are less fearful; they wait till they feel pain, whilst others of more sensibility anticipate it, and suffer in the fear of the pang more acutely than in the pang. 'Tis certain that the threat is sometimes more formidable than the stroke, and 't is possible that the beholders suffer more keenly than the victims. Bodily pain is superficial, seated usually in the skin and the extremities, for the sake of giving us warning to put us on our guard; not in the vitals, where the rupture that produces death is perhaps not felt, and the victim never knew what hurt him. Pain is superficial, and therefore fear is. The torments of martyrdoms are probably most keenly felt by the by-standers. The torments are illusory. The first suffering is the last suffering, the later hurts being lost on insensibility. Our affections and wishes for the external welfare of the hero tumultuously rush to expression in tears and outcries; but we, like him, subside into indifferency and defiance when we perceive how short is the longest arm of malice, how serene is the sufferer.

It is plain that there is no separate essence called
courage, no cup or cell in the brain, no vessel in
the heart containing drops or atoms that make or
give this virtue; but it is the right or healthy state
of every man, when he is free to do that which is
constitutional to him to do. It is directness, — the
instant performing of that which he ought. The
thoughtful man says, You differ from me in opinion
and methods, but do you not see that I cannot think
or act otherwise than I do? that my way of living
is organic? And to be really strong we must
adhere to our own means. On organic action all
strength depends. Hear what women say of doing
a task by sheer force of will : it costs them a fit of
sickness. Plutarch relates that the Pythoness who
tried to prophesy without command in the Temple
at Delphi, though she performed the usual rites,
and inhaled the air of the cavern standing on the
tripod, fell into convulsions and died. Undoubtedly
there is a temperamental courage, a warlike blood,
which loves a fight, does not feel itself except in a
quarrel, as one sees in wasps, or ants, or cocks, or
cats. The like vein appears in certain races of men
and in individuals of every race. In every school
there are certain fighting boys; in every society, the
contradicting men ; in every town, bravoes and
bullies, better or worse dressed, fancy-men, patrons
of the cock-pit and the ring. Courage is temper-

amental, scientific, ideal. Swedenborg has left this
record of his king: " Charles XII. of Sweden did
not know what that was which others called fear, nor
what that spurious valor and daring that is excited
by inebriating draughts, for he never tasted any
liquid but pure water. Of him we may say that
he led a life more remote from death, and in fact
lived more, than any other man." It was told of
the Prince of Condé that " there not being a more
furious man in the world, danger in fight never dis-
turbs him more than just to make him civil, and to
command in words of great obligation to his officers
and men, and without any the least disturbance to
his judgment or spirit." Each has his own courage,
as his own talent; but the courage of the tiger is
one, and of the horse another. The dog that scorns
to fight, will fight for his master. The llama that
will carry a load if you caress him, will refuse food
and die if he is scourged. The fury of onset is one,
and of calm endurance another. There is a courage
of the cabinet as well as a courage of the field; a
courage of manners in private assemblies, and another in public assemblies; a courage which enables
one man to speak masterly to a hostile company,
whilst another man who can easily face a cannon's
mouth dares not open his own.

There is a courage of a merchant in dealing with
his trade, by which dangerous turns of affairs are

met and prevailed over. Merchants recognize as much gallantry, well judged too, in the conduct of a wise and upright man of business in difficult times, as soldiers in a soldier.

There is a courage in the treatment of every art by a master in architecture, in sculpture, in painting, or in poetry, each cheering the mind of the spectator or receiver as by true strokes of genius, which yet nowise implies the presence of physical valor in the artist. This is the courage of genius, in every kind. A certain quantity of power belongs to a certain quantity of faculty. The beautiful voice at church goes sounding on, and covers up in its volume, as in a cloak, all the defects of the choir. The singers, I observe, all yield to it, and so the fair singer indulges her instinct, and dares, and dares, because she knows she can.

It gives the cutting edge to every profession. The judge puts his mind to the tangle of contradictions in the case, squarely accosts the question, and by not being afraid of it, by dealing with it as business which must be disposed of, he sees presently that common arithmetic and common methods apply to this affair. Perseverance strips it of all peculiarity, and ranges it on the same ground as other business. Morphy played a daring game in chess: the daring was only an illusion of the spectator, for the player sees his move to be well forti-

fied and safe. You may see the same dealing in
criticism ; a new book astonishes for a few days,
takes itself out of common jurisdiction, and nobody
knows what to say of it : but the scholar is not deceived. The old principles which books exist to
express are more beautiful than any book; and out
of love of the reality he is an expert judge how far
the book has approached it and where it has come
short. In all applications it is the same power, —
the habit of reference to one's own mind, as the
home of all truth and counsel, and which can easily
dispose of any book because it can very well do
without all books. When a confident man comes
into a company magnifying this or that author he
has freshly read, the company grow silent and
ashamed of their ignorance. But I remember the
old professor, whose searching mind engraved every
word he spoke on the memory of the class, when
we asked if he had read this or that shining novelty, " No, I have never read that book ; " instantly
the book lost credit, and was not to be heard of
again.

Every creature has a courage of his constitution
fit for his duties : — Archimedes, the courage of a
geometer to stick to his diagram, heedless of the
siege and sack of the city ; and the Roman soldier
his faculty to strike at Archimedes. Each is strong,
relying on his own, and each is betrayed when he
seeks in himself the courage of others.

Captain John Brown, the hero of Kansas, said
to me in conversation, that "for a settler in a new
country, one good, believing, strong-minded man is
worth a hundred, nay, a thousand men without
character; and that the right men will give a permanent direction to the fortunes of a state. As
for the bullying drunkards of which armies are
usually made up, he thought cholera, small-pox,
and consumption as valuable recruits." He held
the belief that courage and chastity are silent con-
cerning themselves. He said, "As soon as I hear
one of my men say, 'Ah, let me only get my eye
on such a man, I'll bring him down,' I don't expect
much aid in the fight from that talker. 'T is the
quiet, peaceable men, the men of principle, that
make the best soldiers."

> "'T is still observed those men most valiant are
> Who are most modest ere they came to war."

True courage is not ostentatious; men who wish
to inspire terror seem thereby to confess themselves
cowards. Why do they rely on it, but because
they know how potent it is with themselves?

The true temper has genial influences. It makes
a bond of union between enemies. Governor Wise
of Virginia, in the record of his first interviews
with his prisoner, appeared to great advantage. If
Governor Wise is a superior man, or inasmuch as

he is a superior man, he distinguishes John Brown. As they confer, they understand each other swiftly; each respects the other. If opportunity allowed, they would prefer each other's society and desert their former companions. Enemies would become affectionate. Hector and Achilles, Richard and Saladin, Wellington and Soult, General Daumas and Abdel Kader, become aware that they are nearer and more alike than any other two, and, if their nation and circumstance did not keep them apart, would run into each other's arms.

See too what good contagion belongs to it. Everywhere it finds its own with magnetic affinity. Courage of the soldier awakes the courage of woman. Florence Nightingale brings lint and the blessing of her shadow. Heroic women offer themselves as nurses of the brave veteran. The troop of Virginian infantry that had marched to guard the prison of John Brown ask leave to pay their respects to the prisoner. Poetry and eloquence catch the hint, and soar to a pitch unknown before. Everything feels the new breath except the old doting nigh-dead politicians, whose heart the trumpet of resurrection could not wake.

The charm of the best courages is that they are inventions, inspirations, flashes of genius. The hero could not have done the feat at another hour, in a lower mood. The best act of the marvellous genius of Greece was its first act; not in the statue or the Parthenon, but in the instinct which, at Thermopylæ, held Asia at bay, kept Asia out of Europe, — Asia with its antiquities and organic slavery, — from corrupting the hope and new morning of the West. The statue, the architecture, were the later and inferior creation of the same genius. In view of this moment of history, we recognize a certain prophetic instinct, better than wisdom. Napoleon said well, " My hand is immediately connected with my head;" but the *sacred* courage is connected with the heart. The head is a half, a fraction, until it is enlarged and inspired by the moral sentiment. For it is not the means on which we draw, as health or wealth, practical skill or dexterous talent, or multitudes of followers, that count, but the aims only. The aim reacts back on the means. A great aim aggrandizes the means. The meal and water that are the commissariat of the *forlorn hope* that stake their lives to defend the pass are sacred as the Holy Grail, or as if one had eyes to see in chemistry the fuel that is rushing to feed the sun.

There is a persuasion in the soul of man that he is here for cause, that he was put down in this place by the Creator to do the work for which he inspires him, that thus he is an overmatch for all antagonists that could combine against him. The

pious Mrs. Hutchinson says of some passages in
the defence of Nottingham against the Cavaliers,
" It was a great instruction that the best and highest courages are beams of the Almighty." And
whenever the religious sentiment is adequately af-
firmed, it must be with dazzling courage. As long
as it is cowardly insinuated, as with the wish to
succor some partial and temporary interest, or to
make it affirm some pragmatical tenet which our
parish church receives to-day, it is not imparted,
and cannot inspire or create. For it is always new,
leads and surprises, and practice never comes up
with it. There are ever appearing in the world
men who, almost as soon as they are born, take a
bee-line to the rack of the inquisitor, the axe of
the tyrant, like Giordano Bruno, Vanini, Huss,
Paul, Jesus, and Socrates. Look at Fox's Lives
of the Martyrs, Sewel's History of the Quakers,
Southey's Book of the Church, at the folios of the
Brothers Bollandi, who collected the lives of twen-
ty-five thousand martyrs, confessors, ascetics, and
self-tormentors. There is much of fable, but a
broad basis of fact. The tender skin does not
shrink from bayonets, the timid woman is not
scared by fagots ; the rack is not frightful, nor the
rope ignominious. The poor Puritan, Antony Par-
sons, at the stake, tied straw on his head when the
fire approached him, and said, " This is God's hat."

Sacred courage indicates that a man loves an idea better than all things in the world; that he is aiming neither at pelf or comfort, but will venture all to put in act the invisible thought in his mind. He is everywhere a liberator, but of a freedom that is ideal; not seeking to have land or money or conveniences, but to have no other limitation than that which his own constitution imposes. He is free to speak truth; he is not free to lie. He wishes to break every yoke all over the world which hinders his brother from acting after his thought.

There are degrees of courage, and each step upward makes us acquainted with a higher virtue. Let us say then frankly that the education of the will is the object of our existence. Poverty, the prison, the rack, the fire, the hatred and execrations of our fellow-men, appear trials beyond the endurance of common humanity; but to the hero whose intellect is aggrandized by the soul, and so measures these penalties against the good which his thought surveys, these terrors vanish as darkness at sunrise.

We have little right in piping times of peace to pronounce on these rare heights of character; but there is no assurance of security. In the most private life, difficult duty is never far off. Therefore we must think with courage. Scholars and think-

ers are prone to an effeminate habit, and shrink
if a coarser shout comes up from the street, or a
brutal act is recorded in the journals. The Medical College piles up in its museum its grim monsters of morbid anatomy, and there are melancholy
skeptics with a taste for carrion who batten on
the hideous facts in history, — persecutions, inqui-
sitions, St. Bartholomew massacres, devilish lives,
Nero, Cæsar, Borgia, Marat, Lopez; men in whom
every ray of humanity was extinguished, parricides,
matricides, and whatever moral monsters. These
are not cheerful facts, but they do not disturb a
healthy mind; they require of us a patience as robust as the energy that attacks us, and an unrest-
ing exploration of final causes. Wolf, snake, and
crocodile are not inharmonious in nature, but are
made useful as checks, scavengers, and pioneers;
and we must have a scope as large as Nature's to
deal with beast-like men, detect what scullion func-
tion is assigned them, and foresee in the secular
melioration of the planet how these will become
unnecessary and will die out.

He has not learned the lesson of life who does
not every day surmount a fear. I do not wish to
put myself or any man into a theatrical position,
or urge him to ape the courage of his comrade.
Have the courage not to adopt another's courage.
There is scope and cause and resistance enough for

us in our proper work and circumstance. And there is no creed of an honest man, be he Christian, Turk, or Gentoo, which does not equally preach it. If you have no faith in beneficent power above you, but see only an adamantine fate coiling its folds about nature and man, then reflect that the best use of fate is to teach us courage, if only because baseness cannot change the appointed event. If you accept your thoughts as inspirations from the Supreme Intelligence, obey them when they prescribe difficult duties, because they come only so long as they are used; or, if your skepticism reaches to the last verge, and you have no confidence in any foreign mind, then be brave, because there is one good opinion which must always be of consequence to you, namely, your own.

———

I am permitted to enrich my chapter by adding an anecdote of pure courage from real life, as narrated in a ballad by a lady to whom all the particulars of the fact are exactly known.

GEORGE NIDIVER.

Men have done brave deeds,
  And bards have sung them well:
I of good George Nidiver
  Now the tale will tell.

In Californian mountains
  A hunter bold was he :
Keen his eye and sure his aim
  As any you should see.

A little Indian boy
  Followed him everywhere,
Eager to share the hunter's joy,
  The hunter's meal to share.

And when the bird or deer
  Fell by the hunter's skill,
The boy was always near
  To help with right good-will.

One day as through the cleft
  Between two mountains steep,
Shut in both right and left,
  Their questing way they keep,

They see two grizzly bears
  With hunger fierce and fell
Rush at them unawares
  Right down the narrow dell.

The boy turned round with screams,
  And ran with terror wild ;
One of the pair of savage beasts
  Pursued the shrieking child.

The hunter raised his gun, —
  He knew *one* charge was all, —
And through the boy's pursuing foe
  He sent his only ball.

The other on George Nidiver
  Came on with dreadful pace:
The hunter stood unarmed,
  And met him face to face.

I say *unarmed* he stood.
  Against those frightful paws
The rifle butt, or club of wood,
  Could stand no more than straws.

George Nidiver stood still
  And looked him in the face ;
The wild beast stopped amazed,
  Then came with slackening pace.

Still firm the hunter stood,
  Although his heart beat high ;
Again the creature stopped,
  And gazed with wondering eye.

The hunter met his gaze,
  Nor yet an inch gave way;
The bear turned slowly round,
  And slowly moved away.

What thoughts were in his mind
  It would be hard to spell :
What thoughts were in George **Nidiver**
  I rather guess than tell.

But sure that rifle's aim,
  Swift choice of generous part,
Showed in its passing gleam
  The depths of a brave heart.

SUCCESS.

SUCCESS.

Our American people cannot be taxed with slowness in performance or in praising their performance. The earth is shaken by our engineries. We are feeling our youth and nerve and bone. We have the power of territory and of sea-coast, and know the use of these. We count our census, we read our growing valuations, we survey our map, which becomes old in a year or two. Our eyes run approvingly along the lengthened lines of railroad and telegraph. We have gone nearest to the Pole. We have discovered the Antartic continent. We interfere in Central and South America, at Canton, and in Japan; we are adding to an already enormous territory. Our political constitution is the hope of the world, and we value ourselves on all these feats.

'T is the way of the world; 't is the law of youth, and of unfolding strength. Men are made each with some triumphant superiority, which, through some adaptation of fingers or ear or eye or ciphering or pugilistic or musical or literary

craft, enriches the community with a new art; and
not only we, but all men of European stock, value
these certificates. Giotto could draw a perfect circle: Erwin of Steinbach could build a minster;
Olaf, king of Norway, could run round his galley
on the blades of the oars of the rowers when the
ship was in motion; Ojeda could run out swiftly
on a plank projected from the top of a tower, turn
round swiftly and come back; Evelyn writes from
Rome: "Bernini, the Florentine sculptor, architect,
painter and poet, a little before my coming to
Rome, gave a public opera, wherein he painted the
scenes, cut the statues, invented the engines, composed the music, writ the comedy and built the
theatre."

"There is nothing in war," said Napoleon,
"which I cannot do by my own hands. If there is
nobody to make gunpowder, I can manufacture it.
The gun-carriages I know how to construct. If it
is necessary to make cannons at the forge, I can
make them. The details of working them in battle, if it is necessary to teach, I shall teach them.
In administration, it is I alone who have arranged
the finances, as you know."

It is recorded of Linnæus, among many proofs of
his beneficent skill, that when the timber in the
ship-yards of Sweden was ruined by rot, Linnæus
was desired by the government to find a remedy.

He studied the insects that infested the timber, and found that they laid their eggs in the logs within certain days in April, and he directed that during ten days at that season the logs should be immersed under water in the docks; which being done, the timber was found to be uninjured.

Columbus at Veragua found plenty of gold; but leaving the coast, the ship full of one hundred and fifty skilful seamen, — some of them old pilots, and with too much experience of their craft and treachery to him, — the wise admiral kept his private record of his homeward path. And when he reached Spain he told the King and Queen that " they may ask all the pilots who came with him where is Veragua. Let them answer and say if they know where Veragua lies. I assert that they can give no other account than that they went to lands where there was abundance of gold, but they do not know the way to return thither, but would be obliged to go on a voyage of discovery as much as if they had never been there before. There is a mode of reckoning," he proudly adds, " derived from astronomy, which is sure and safe to any one who understands it."

Hippocrates in Greece knew how to stay the devouring plague which ravaged Athens in his time, and his skill died with him. Dr. Benjamin Rush, in Philadelphia, carried that city heroically through the yellow fever of the year 1793. Leverrier carried the Copernican system in his head, and knew where to look for the new planet. We have seen an American woman write a novel of which a million copies were sold, in all languages, and which had one merit, of speaking to the universal heart, and was read with equal interest to three audiences, namely, in the parlor, in the kitchen, and in the nursery of every house. We have seen women who could institute hospitals and schools in armies. We have seen a woman who by pure song could melt the souls of whole populations. And there is no limit to these varieties of talent.

These are arts to be thankful for, — each one as it is a new direction of human power. We cannot choose but respect them. Our civilization is made up of a million contributions of this kind. For success, to be sure we esteem it a test in other people, since we do first in ourselves. We respect ourselves more if we have succeeded. Neither do we grudge to each of these benefactors the praise or the profit which accrues from his industry.

Here are already quite different degrees of moral merit in these examples. I don't know but we and our race elsewhere set a higher value on wealth, victory, and coarse superiority of all kinds, than other men, — have less tranquillity of mind, are less easily contented. The Saxon is taught from his in-

fancy to wish to be first. The Norseman was a rest-
less rider, fighter, freebooter. The ancient Norse
ballads describe him as afflicted with this inextin-
guishable thirst of victory. The mother says to her
son : —

> " Success shall be in thy courser tall,
> Success in thyself, which is best of all,
> Success in thy hand, success in thy foot,
> In struggle with man, in battle with brute : —
> The holy God and Saint Drothin dear
> Shall never shut eyes on thy career ;
>   Look out, look out, Svend Vonved ! "

These feats that we extol do not signify so much
as we say. These boasted arts are of very recent
origin. They are local conveniences, but do not
really add to our stature. The greatest men of the
world have managed not to want them. Newton
was a great man, without telegraph, or gas, or
steam-coach, or rubber shoes, or lucifer-matches, or
ether for his pain ; so was Shakspeare, and Alfred,
and Scipio, and Socrates. These are local conveniences, but how easy to go now to parts of the world
where not only all these arts are wanting, but where
they are despised. The Arabian sheiks, the most
dignified people in the planet, do not want them ;
yet have as much self-respect as the English, and
are easily able to impress the Frenchman or the
American who visits them with the respect due to
a brave and sufficient man.

These feats have to be sure great difference of
merit, and some of them involve power of a high
kind.   But the public values the invention more
than the inventor does.   The inventor knows there
is much more and better where this came from.
The public sees in it a lucrative secret.   Men see
the reward which the inventor enjoys, and they
think, 'How shall we win that?'   Cause and effect
are a little tedious; how to leap to the result by
short or by false means?   We are not scrupulous.
What we ask is victory, without regard to the cause;
after the Rob Roy rule, after the Napoleon rule, to
be the strongest to-day, — the way of the Talley-
rands, prudent people, whose watches go faster
than their neighbors', and who detect the first moment of decline and throw themselves on the instant
on the winning side.   I have heard that Nelson
used to say, "Never mind the justice or the impu-
dence, only let me succeed."   Lord Brougham's single duty of counsel is, " to get the prisoner clear."
Fuller says 't is a maxim of lawyers that "a crown
once worn cleareth all defects of the wearer thereof."
Rien ne réussit mieux que le succès.   And we
Americans are tainted with this insanity, as our
bankruptcies and our reckless politics may show.
We are great by exclusion, grasping, and egotism.
Our success takes from all what it gives to one.
'T is a haggard, malignant, careworn running for
luck.

Egotism is a kind of buckram that gives momentary strength and concentration to men, and seems
to be much used in nature for fabrics in which local
and spasmodic energy is required. I could point to
men in this country, of indispensable importance to
the carrying on of American life, of this humor,
whom we could ill spare; any one of them would be
a national loss. But it spoils conversation. They
will not try conclusions with you. They are ever
thrusting this pampered self between you and them.
It is plain they have a long education to undergo
to reach simplicity and plain - dealing, which are
what a wise man mainly cares for in his companion.
Nature knows how to convert evil to good; Nature
utilizes misers, fanatics, show-men, egotists, to accomplish her ends; but we must not think better
of the foible for that. The passion for sudden
success is rude and puerile, just as war, cannons,
and executions are used to clear the ground of bad,
lumpish, irreclaimable savages, but always to the
damage of the conquerors.

I hate this shallow Americanism which hopes to
get rich by credit, to get knowledge by raps on
midnight tables, to learn the economy of the mind
by phrenology, or skill without study, or mastery
without apprenticeship, or the sale of goods through
pretending that they sell, or power through making
believe you are powerful, or through a packed jury

or caucus, bribery and "repeating" votes, or wealth
by fraud. They think they have got it, but they
have got something else, — a crime which calls for
another crime, and another devil behind that; these
are steps to suicide, infamy, and the harming of
mankind. We countenance each other in this life
of show, puffing, advertisement, and manufacture
of public opinion; and excellence is lost sight of
in the hunger for sudden performance and praise.

There was a wise man, an Italian artist, Michel
Angelo, who writes thus of himself : " Meanwhile
the Cardinal Ippolito, in whom all my best hopes
were placed, being dead, I began to understand that
the promises of this world are for the most part
vain phantoms, and that to confide in one's self, and
become something of worth and value, is the best
and safest course." Now, though I am by no
means sure that the reader will assent to all my
propositions, yet I think we shall agree in my first
rule for success, — that we shall drop the brag and
the advertisement, and take Michel Angelo's course,
" to confide in one's self, and be something of worth
and value."

Each man has an aptitude born with him. Do
your work. I have to say this often, but nature
says it oftener. 'T is clownish to insist on doing
all with one's own hands, as if every man should
build his own clumsy house, forge his hammer, and

bake his dough; but he is to dare to do what he can do best; not help others as they would direct him, but as he knows his helpful power to be. To do otherwise is to neutralize all those extraordinary special talents distributed among men. Yet whilst this self-truth is essential to the exhibition of the world and to the growth and glory of each mind, it is rare to find a man who believes his own thought or who speaks that which he was created to say. As nothing astonishes men so much as common-sense and plain dealing, so nothing is more rare in any man than an act of his own. Any work looks wonderful to him, except that which he can do. We do not believe our own thought; we must serve somebody; we must quote somebody; we dote on the old and the distant; we are tickled by great names; we import the religion of other nations; we quote their opinions; we cite their laws. The gravest and learnedest courts in this country shudder to face a new question, and will wait months and years for a case to occur that can be tortured into a precedent, and thus throw on a bolder party the *onus* of an initiative. Thus we do not carry a counsel in our breasts, or do not know it; and because we cannot shake off from our shoes this dust of Europe and Asia, the world seems to be born old, society is under a spell, every man is a borrower and a mimic, life is theatrical and literature a quotation;

and hence that depression of spirits, that furrow of care, said to mark every American brow.

Self-trust is the first secret of success, the belief that if you are here the authorities of the universe put you here, and for cause, or with some task strictly appointed you in your constitution, and so long as you work at that you are well and successful. It by no means consists in rushing prematurely to a showy feat that shall catch the eye and satisfy spectators. It is enough if you work in the right direction. So far from the performance being the real success, it is clear that the success was much earlier than that, namely, when all the feats that make our civility were the thoughts of good heads. The fame of each discovery rightly attaches to the mind that made the formula which contains all the details, and not to the manufacturers who now make their gain by it; although the mob uniformly cheers the publisher, and not the inventor. It is the dulness of the multitude that they cannot see the house in the ground-plan; the working, in the model of the projector. Whilst it is a thought, though it were a new fuel, or a new food, or the creation of agriculture, it is cried down, it is a chimera; but when it is a fact, and comes in the shape of eight per cent, ten per cent, a hundred per cent, they cry, 'It is the voice of God.' Horatio Greenough the sculptor said to me of Robert Fulton's visit to Paris : "Fulton knocked at the door of Napoleon with steam, and was rejected ; and Napoleon lived long enough to know that he had excluded a greater power than his own."

Is there no loving of knowledge, and of art, and of our design, for itself alone ? Cannot we please ourselves with performing our work, or gaining truth and power, without being praised for it ? I gain my point, I gain all points, if I can reach my companion with any statement which teaches him his own worth. The sum of wisdom is, that the time is never lost that is devoted to work. The good workman never says, 'There, that will do ;' but, 'There, that is it: try it, and come again, it will last always.' If the artist, in whatever art, is well at work on his own design, it signifies little that he does not yet find orders or customers. I pronounce that young man happy who is content with having acquired the skill which he had aimed at, and waits willingly when the occasion of making it appreciated shall arrive, knowing well that it will not loiter. The time your rival spends in dressing up his work for effect, hastily, and for the market, you spend in study and experiments towards real knowledge and efficiency. He has thereby sold his picture or machine, or won the prize, or got the appointment ; but you have raised yourself into a higher school of art, and a few years will show the advantage of the real master over the short popularity of the showman. I know it is a nice point to discriminate this self-trust, which is the pledge of all mental vigor and performance, from the disease to which it is allied, — the exaggeration of the part which we can play ; — yet they are two things. But it is sanity to know that, over my talent or knack, and a million times better than any talent, is the central intelligence which subordinates and uses all talents ; and it is only as a door into this, that any talent or the knowledge it gives is of value. He only who comes into this central intelligence, in which no egotism or exaggeration can be, comes into self-possession.

My next point is that in the scale of powers it is not talent but sensibility which is best : talent confines, but the central life puts us in relation to all. How often it seems the chief good to be born with a cheerful temper and well adjusted to the tone of the human race. Such a man feels himself in harmony, and conscious by his receptivity of an infinite strength. Like Alfred, " good fortune accompanies him like a gift of God." Feel yourself, and be not daunted by things. 'T is the fulness of man that runs over into objects, and makes his Bibles and Shakspeares and Homers so great. The joyful reader borrows of his own ideas to fill their faulty outline, and knows not that he borrows and gives.

There is something of poverty in our criticism. We assume that there are few great men, all the rest are little; that there is but one Homer, but one Shakspeare, one Newton, one Socrates. But the soul in her beaming hour does not acknowledge these usurpations. We should know how to praise Socrates, or Plato, or Saint John, without impoverishing us. In good hours we do not find Shakspeare or Homer over-great, only to have been translators of the happy present, and every man and woman divine possibilities. 'T is the good reader that makes the good book; a good head cannot read amiss, in every book he finds passages which seem confidences or asides hidden from all else and unmistakably meant for his ear.

The light by which we see in this world comes out from the soul of the observer. Wherever any noble sentiment dwelt, it made the faces and houses around to shine. Nay, the powers of this busy brain are miraculous and illimitable. Therein are the rules and formulas by which the whole empire of matter is worked. There is no prosperity, trade, art, city, or great material wealth of any kind, but if you trace it home you will find it rooted in a thought of some individual man.

Is all life a surface affair? 'T is curious, but our difference of wit appears to be only a difference of impressionability, or power to appreciate

faint, fainter, and infinitely faintest voices and vis-
ions. When the scholar or the writer has pumped
his brain for thoughts and verses, and then comes
abroad into Nature, has he never found that there
is a better poetry hinted in a boy's whistle of a
tune, or in the piping of a sparrow, than in all
his literary results? We call it health. What is
so admirable as tho health of youth? — with his
long days because his eyes are good, and brisk cir-
culations keep him warm in cold rooms, and he
loves books that speak to the imagination ; and he
can read Plato, covered to his chin with a cloak in
a cold upper chamber, though he should associate
the Dialogues ever after with a woollen smell. 'T is
the bane of life that natural effects are continually
crowded out, and artificial arrangements substi-
tuted. We remember when in early youth the
earth spoke and the heavens glowed ; when an
evening, any evening, grim and wintry, sleet and
snow, was enough for us ; the houses were in the
air. Now it costs a rare combination of clouds
and lights to overcome the common and mean.
What is it we look for in the landscape, in sunsets
and sunrises, in the sea and the firmament? what
but a compensation for the cramp and pettiness of
human performances? We bask in the day, and
the mind finds somewhat as great as itself. In Nature all is large massive repose. Remember what

befalls a city boy who goes for the first time into the October woods. He is suddenly initiated into a pomp and glory that brings to pass for him the dreams of romance. He is the king he dreamed he was; he walks through tents of gold, through bowers of crimson, porphyry and topaz, pavilion on pavilion, garlanded with vines, flowers and sunbeams, with incense and music, with so many hints to his astonished senses; the leaves twinkle and pique and flatter him, and his eye and step are tempted on by what hazy distances to happier solitudes. All this happiness he owes only to his finer perception. The owner of the wood-lot finds only a number of discolored trees, and says, ' They ought to come down; they are n't growing any better; they should be cut and corded before spring.'

Wordsworth writes of the delights of the boy in Nature : —

" For never will come back the hour
  Of splendor in the grass, of glory in the flower."

But I have just seen a man, well knowing what he spoke of, who told me that the verse was not true for him; that his eyes opened as he grew older, and that every spring was more beautiful to him than the last.

We live among gods of our own creation. Does that deep-toned bell, which has shortened many a night of ill nerves, render to you nothing but acous-

tic vibrations? Is the old church which gave you
the first lessons of religious life, or the village
school, or the college where you first knew the
dreams of fancy and joys of thought, only boards
or brick and mortar? Is the house in which you
were born, or the house in which your dearest
friend lived, only a piece of real estate whose value
is covered by the Hartford insurance? You walk
on the beach and enjoy the animation of the picture. Scoop up a little water in the hollow of your
palm, take up a handful of shore sand; well, these
are the elements. What is the beach but acres of
sand? what is the ocean but cubic miles of water?
a little more or less signifies nothing. No, it is
that this brute matter is part of somewhat not
brute. It is that the sand floor is held by spheral
gravity, and bent to be a part of the round globe,
under the optical sky, — part of the astonishing astronomy, and existing at last to moral ends and
from moral causes.

The world is not made up to the eye of figures,
that is, only half; it is also made of color. How
that element washes the universe with its enchanting waves! The sculptor had ended his work, and
behold a new world of dream-like glory. 'T is the
last stroke of Nature; beyond color she cannot go.
In like manner, life is made up, not of knowledge
only, but of love also. If thought is form, senti-

ment is color. It clothes the skeleton world with space, variety, and glow. The hues of sunset make life great; so the affections make some little web of cottage and fireside populous, important, and filling the main space in our history.

The fundamental fact in our metaphysic constitution is the correspondence of man to the world, so that every change in that writes a record in the mind. The mind yields sympathetically to the tendencies or law which stream through things and make the order of nature; and in the perfection of this correspondence or expressiveness, the health and force of man consist. If we follow this hint into our intellectual education, we shall find that it is not propositions, not new dogmas and a logical exposition of the world that are our first need; but to watch and tenderly cherish the intellectual and moral sensibilities, those fountains of right thought, and woo them to stay and make their home with us. Whilst they abide with us we shall not think amiss. Our perception far outruns our talent. We bring a welcome to the highest lessons of religion and of poetry out of all proportion beyond our skill to teach. And, further, the great hearing and sympathy of men is more true and wise than their speaking is wont to be. A deep sympathy is what we require for any student of the mind; for the chief difference between man and man is a difference of impressionability. Aristotle or Bacon or Kant propound some maxim which is the key-note of philosophy thenceforward. But I am more interested to know that when at last they have hurled out their grand word, it is only some familiar experience of every man in the street. If it be not, it will never be heard of again.

Ah! if one could keep this sensibility, and live in the happy sufficing present, and find the day and its cheap means contenting, which only ask receptivity in you, and no strained exertion and cankering ambition, overstimulating to be at the head of your class and the head of society, and to have distinction and laurels and consumption! We are not strong by our power to penetrate, but by our relatedness. The world is enlarged for us, not by new objects, but by finding more affinities and potencies in those we have.

This sensibility appears in the homage to beauty which exalts the faculties of youth; in the power which form and color exert upon the soul; when we see eyes that are a compliment to the human race, features that explain the Phidian sculpture. Fontenelle said: "There are three things about which I have curiosity, though I know nothing of them, — music, poetry, and love." The great doctors of this science are the greatest men, — Dante, Petrarch, Michel Angelo and Shakspeare. The wise Socrates treats this matter with a certain archness, yet with very marked expressions. "I am always," he says, "asserting that I happen to know, I may say, nothing but a mere trifle relating to matters of love; yet in that kind of learning I lay claim to being more skilled than any one man of the past or present time." They may well speak in this uncertain manner of their knowledge, and in this confident manner of their will, for the secret of it is hard to detect, so deep it is; and yet genius is measured by its skill in this science.

Who is he in youth or in maturity or even in old age, who does not like to hear of those sensibilities which turn curled heads round at church, and send wonderful eye-beams across assemblies, from one to one, never missing in the thickest crowd? The keen statist reckons by tens and hundreds; the genial man is interested in every slipper that comes into the assembly. The passion, alike everywhere, creeps under the snows of Scandinavia, under the fires of the equator, and swims in the seas of Polynesia. Lofn is as puissant a divinity in the Norse Edda as Camadeva in the red vault of India, Eros in the Greek, or Cupid in the Latin heaven. And what is specially true of love is that it is a state of extreme impressionability; the lover has more senses and finer senses than others; his eye and ear are telegraphs; he reads omens on the flower, and cloud, and face, and form, and gesture, and reads them aright. In his surprise at the sudden and entire understanding that is between him and the beloved person, it occurs to him that they might somehow meet independently of time and place. How delicious the belief that he could elude all guards, precautions, ceremonies, means, and delays, and hold instant and sempiternal communication! In solitude, in banishment, the hope returned, and the experiment was eagerly tried. The supernal powers seem to take his part. What was on his lips to say is uttered by his friend. When he went abroad, he met, by wonderful casualties, the one person he sought. If in his walk he chanced to look back, his friend was walking behind him. And it has happened that the artist has often drawn in his pictures the face of the future wife whom he had not yet seen.

But also in complacencies nowise so strict as this of the passion, the man of sensibility counts it a delight only to hear a child's voice fully addressed to him, or to see the beautiful manners of the youth of either sex. When the event is past and remote, how insignificant the greatest compared with the piquancy of the present! To-day at the school examination the professor interrogates Sylvina in the history class about Odoacer and Alaric.

Sylvina can't remember, but suggests that Odoacer was defeated; and the professor tartly replies, "No, he defeated the Romans." But 't is plain to the visitor that 't is of no importance at all about Odoacer and 't is a great deal of importance about Sylvina, and if she says he was defeated, why he had better a great deal have been defeated than give her a moment's annoy. Odoacer, if there was a particle of the gentleman in him, would have said, Let me be defeated a thousand times.

And as our tenderness for youth and beauty gives a new and just importance to their fresh and manifold claims, so the like sensibility gives welcome to all excellence, has eyes and hospitality for merit in corners. An Englishman of marked character and talent, who had brought with him hither one or two friends and a library of mystics, assured me that nobody and nothing of possible interest was left in England, — he had brought all that was alive away. I was forced to reply: "No, next door to you probably, on the other side of the partition in the same house, was a greater man than any you had seen." Every man has a history worth knowing, if he could tell it, or if we could draw it from him. Character and wit have their own magnetism. Send a deep man into any town, and he will find another deep man there, unknown hitherto to his neighbors. That is the great happiness of life,

— to add to our high acquaintances. The very law of averages might have assured you that there will be in every hundred heads, say ten or five good heads. Morals are generated as the atmosphere is. 'T is a secret, the genesis of either; but the springs of justice and courage do not fail any more than salt or sulphur springs.

The world is always opulent, the oracles are never silent; but the receiver must by a happy temperance be brought to that top of condition, that frolic health, that he can easily take and give these fine communications. Health is the condition of wisdom, and the sign is cheerfulness, — an open and noble temper. There was never poet who had not the heart in the right place. The old trouveur, Pons Capdueil, wrote, —

> "Oft have I heard, and deem the witness true,
>   Whom man delights in, God delights in too."

All beauty warms the heart, is a sign of health, prosperity, and the favor of God. Everything lasting and fit for men the Divine Power has marked with this stamp. What delights, what emancipates, not what scares and pains us is wise and good in speech and in the arts. For, truly, the heart at the centre of the universe with every throb hurls the flood of happiness into every artery, vein, and veinlet, so that the whole system is inundated with the tides of joy. The plenty of the poorest place is too great: the harvest cannot be gathered. Every sound ends in music. The edge of every surface is tinged with prismatic rays.

One more trait of true success. The good mind chooses what is positive, what is advancing, — embraces the affirmative. Our system is one of poverty. 'T is presumed, as I said, there is but one Shakspeare, one Homer, one Jesus, — not that all are or shall be inspired. But we must begin by affirming. Truth and goodness subsist forevermore. It is true there is evil and good, night and day: but these are not equal. The day is great and final. The night is for the day, but the day is not for the night. What is this immortal demand for more, which belongs to our constitution? this enormous ideal? There is no such critic and beggar as this terrible Soul. No historical person begins to content us. We know the satisfactoriness of justice, the sufficiency of truth. We know the answer that leaves nothing to ask. We know the Spirit by its victorious tone. The searching tests to apply to every new pretender are amount and quality, — what does he add? and what is the state of mind he leaves me in? Your theory is unimportant; but what new stock you can add to humanity, or how high you can carry life? A man is a man only as he makes life and nature happier to us.

I fear the popular notion of success stands in direct opposition in all points to the real and wholesome success. One adores public opinion, the other private opinion; one fame, the other desert; one feats, the other humility; one lucre, the other love; one monopoly, and the other hospitality of mind.

We may apply this affirmative law to letters, to manners, to art, to the decorations of our houses, etc. I do not find executions or tortures or lazar-houses, or grisly photographs of the field on the day after the battle, fit subjects for cabinet pictures. I think that some so-called " sacred subjects " must be treated with more genius than I have seen in the masters of Italian or Spanish art to be right pictures for houses and churches. Nature does not invite such exhibition. Nature lays the ground-plan of each creature accurately, sternly fit for all his functions; then veils it scrupulously. See how carefully she covers up the skeleton. The eye shall not see it; the sun shall not shine on it. She weaves her tissues and integuments of flesh and skin and hair and beautiful colors of the day over it, and forces death down underground, and makes haste to cover it up with leaves and vines, and wipes carefully out every trace by new creation. Who and what are you that would lay the ghastly anatomy bare?

Don't hang a dismal picture on the wall, and do

not daub with sables and glooms in your conversation. Don't be a cynic and disconsolate preacher. Don't bewail and bemoan. Omit the negative propositions. Nerve us with incessant affirmatives. Don't waste yourself in rejection, nor bark against the bad, but chant the beauty of the good. When that is spoken which has a right to be spoken, the chatter and the criticism will stop. Set down nothing that will not help somebody ; —

> "For every gift of noble origin
> Is breathed upon by Hope's perpetual breath."

The affirmative of affirmatives is love. As much love, so much perception. As caloric to matter, so is love to mind; so it enlarges, and so it empowers it. Good-will makes insight, as one finds his way to the sea by embarking on a river. I have seen scores of people who can silence me, but I seek one who shall make me forget or overcome the frigidities and imbecilities into which I fall. The painter Giotto, Vasari tells us, renewed art because he put more goodness into his heads. To awake in man and to raise the sense of worth, to educate his feeling and judgment so that he shall scorn himself for a bad action, that is the only aim.

'T is cheap and easy to destroy. There is not a joyful boy or an innocent girl buoyant with fine purposes of duty, in all the street full of eager and rosy faces, but a cynic can chill and dis-

hearten with a single word. Despondency comes
readily enough to the most sanguine. The cynic
has only to follow their hint with his bitter confirmation, and they check that eager courageous
pace and go home with heavier step and premature age. They will themselves quickly enough
give the hint he wants to the cold wretch. Which
of them has not failed to please where they most
wished it? or blundered where they were most
ambitious of success? or found themselves awkward
or tedious or incapable of study, thought, or heroism, and only hoped by good sense and fidelity to
do what they could and pass unblamed? And this
witty malefactor makes their little hope less with
satire and skepticism, and slackens the springs of
endeavor. Yes, this is easy; but to help the young
soul, add energy, inspire hope and blow the coals
into a useful flame; to redeem defeat by new
thought, by firm action, that is not easy, that is the
work of divine men.

We live on different planes or platforms. There
is an external life, which is educated at school,
taught to read, write, cipher, and trade; taught to
grasp all the boy can get, urging him to put himself forward, to make himself useful and agreeable
in the world, to ride, run, argue and contend, unfold his talents, shine, conquer and possess.

But the inner life sits at home, and does not

learn to do things, nor value these feats at all.
'T is a quiet, wise perception. It loves truth, because it is itself real; it loves right, it knows nothing else; but it makes no progress; was as wise in
our first memory of it as now; is just the same now
in maturity and hereafter in age, it was in youth.
We have grown to manhood and womanhood; we
have powers, connection, children, reputations, professions: this makes no account of them all. It
lives in the great present; it makes the present
great. This tranquil, well - founded, wide - seeing
soul is no express-rider, no attorney, no magistrate:
it lies in the sun and broods on the world. A person of this temper once said to a man of much activity, "I will pardon you that you do so much,
and you me that I do nothing." And Euripides
says that "Zeus hates busybodies and those who
do too much."

OLD AGE.

OLD AGE.

On the anniversary of the Phi Beta Kappa Society at Cambridge in 1861, the venerable President Quincy, senior member of the Society, as well as senior alumnus of the University, was received at the dinner with peculiar demonstrations of respect. He replied to these compliments in a speech, and, gracefully claiming the privileges of a literary society, entered at some length into an Apology for Old Age, and, aiding himself by notes in his hand, made a sort of running commentary on Cicero's chapter " De Senectute." The character of the speaker, the transparent good faith of his praise and blame, and the *naïveté* of his eager preference of Cicero's opinions to King David's, gave unusual interest to the College festival. It was a discourse full of dignity, honoring him who spoke and those who heard.

The speech led me to look over at home — an easy task — Cicero's famous essay, charming by its uniform rhetorical merit; heroic with Stoical precepts, with a Roman eye to the claims of the State;

happiest perhaps in his praise of life on the farm;
and rising at the conclusion to a lofty strain.   But
he does not exhaust the subject; rather invites the
attempt to add traits to the picture from our broader
modern life.

Cicero makes no reference to the illusions which
cling to the element of time, and in which Nature
delights.   Wellington, in speaking of military men,
said, "What masks are these uniforms to hide
cowards!"   I have often detected the like deception in the cloth shoe, wadded pelisse, wig, spectacles and padded chair of Age.   Nature lends
herself to these illusions, and adds dim sight, deaf-
ness, cracked voice, snowy hair, short memory and
sleep.   These also are masks, and all is not Age that
wears them.   Whilst we yet call ourselves young
and our mates are yet youths with even boyish remains, one good fellow in the set prematurely sports
a gray or a bald head, which does not impose on us
who know how innocent of sanctity or of Platonism
he is, but does deceive his juniors and the public,
who presently distinguish him with a most amusing
respect: and this lets us into the secret that the
venerable forms that so awed our childhood were
just such imposters.   Nature is full of freaks, and
now puts an old head on young shoulders, and then
a young heart beating under fourscore winters.

For if the essence of age is not present, these

signs, whether of Art or Nature, are counterfeit
and ridiculous : and the essence of age is intellect.
Wherever that appears, we call it old. If we look
into the eyes of the youngest person we sometimes
discover that here is one who knows already what
you would go about with much pains to teach him ;
there is that in him which is the ancestor of all
around him: which fact the Indian Vedas express
when they say, " He that can discriminate is the
father of his father." And in our old British
legends of Arthur and the Round Table, his friend
and counsellor, Merlin the Wise, is a babe found
exposed in a basket by the river-side, and, though
an infant of only a few days, speaks articulately to
those who discover him, tells his name and history,
and presently foretells the fate of the by-standers.
Wherever there is power, there is age. Don't be
deceived by dimples and curls. I tell you that
babe is a thousand years old.

Time is indeed the theatre and seat of illusion : nothing is so ductile and elastic. The mind
stretches an hour to a century and dwarfs an age
to an hour. Saadi found in a mosque at Damascus
an old Persian of a hundred and fifty years, who
was dying, and was saying to himself, " I said,
coming into the world by birth, ' I will enjoy myself for a few moments.' Alas ! at the variegated
table of life I partook of a few mouthfuls, and the

Fates said, '*Enough!*'" That which does not
decay is so central and controlling in us, that, as
long as one is alone by himself, he is not sensible
of the inroads of time, which always begin at the
surface-edges. If, on a winter day, you should
stand within a bell-glass, the face and color of the
afternoon clouds would not indicate whether it were
June or January; and if we did not find the reflec-
tion of ourselves in the eyes of the young people,
we could not know that the century-clock had
struck seventy instead of twenty. How many men
habitually believe that each chance passenger with
whom they converse is of their own age, and presently find it was his father and not his brother
whom they knew!

But not to press too hard on these deceits and
illusions of Nature, which are inseparable from
our condition, and looking at age under an aspect
more conformed to the common-sense, if the question be the felicity of age, I fear the first popular
judgments will be unfavorable. From the point
of sensuous experience, seen from the streets and
markets and the haunts of pleasure and gain, the
estimate of age is low, melancholy and skeptical.
Frankly face the facts, and see the result. Tobacco, coffee, alcohol, hashish, prussic acid, strych-
nine, are weak dilutions: the surest poison is time.
This cup which Nature puts to our lips, has a won-

derful virtue, surpassing that of any other draught. It opens the senses, adds power, fills us with exalted dreams, which we call hope, love, ambition, science: especially, it creates a craving for larger draughts of itself. But they who take the larger draughts are drunk with it, lose their stature, strength, beauty, and senses, and end in folly and delirium. We postpone our literary work until we have more ripeness and skill to write, and we one day discover that our literary talent was a youthful effervescence which we have now lost. We had a judge in Massachusetts who at sixty proposed to resign, alleging that he perceived a certain decay in his faculties; he was dissuaded by his friends, on account of the public convenience at that time. At seventy it was hinted to him that it was time to retire; but he now replied that he thought his judgment as robust and all his faculties as good as ever they were. But besides the self-deception, the strong and hasty laborers of the street do not work well with the chronic valetudinarian. Youth is everywhere in place. Age, like woman, requires fit surroundings. Age is comely in coaches, in churches, in chairs of state and ceremony, in council-chambers, in courts of justice and historical societies. Age is becoming in the country. But in the rush and uproar of Broadway, if you look into the faces of the passengers there is dejection or in-

dignation in the seniors, a certain concealed sense
of injury, and the lip made up with a heroic determination not to mind it. Few envy the consideration enjoyed by the oldest inhabitant. We do not
count a man's years, until he has nothing else to
count. The vast inconvenience of animal immortality was told in the fable of Tithonus. In short,
the creed of the street is, Old Age is not disgrace-
ful, but immensely disadvantageous. Life is well
enough, but we shall all be glad to get out of it,
and they will all be glad to have us.

This is odious on the face of it. Universal convictions are not to be shaken by the whimseys of
overfed butchers and firemen, or by the sentimental
fears of girls who would keep the infantile bloom
on their cheeks. We know the value of experience. Life and art are cumulative; and he who
has accomplished something in any department
alone deserves to be heard on that subject. A man
of great employments and excellent performance
used to assure me that he did not think a man
worth anything until he was sixty; although this
smacks a little of the resolution of a certain "Young
Men's Republican Club," that all men should be
held eligible who were under seventy. But in all
governments, the councils of power were held by
the old; and patricians or *patres*, senate or *senes*,
seigneurs or seniors, *gerousia*, the senate of

Sparta, the presbytery of the Church, and the like, all signify simply old men.

The cynical creed or lampoon of the market is refuted by the universal prayer for long life, which is the verdict of Nature and justified by all history. We have, it is true, examples of an accelerated pace by which young men achieved grand works; as in the Macedonian Alexander, in Raffaelle, Shakspeare, Pascal, Burns, and Byron; but these are rare exceptions. Nature, in the main, vindicates her law. Skill to do comes of doing; knowledge comes by eyes always open, and working hands; and there is no knowledge that is not power. Béranger said, "Almost all the good workmen live long." And if the life be true and noble, we have quite another sort of seniors than the frowzy, timorous, peevish dotards who are falsely old, — namely, the men who fear no city, but by whom cities stand; who appearing in any street, the people empty their houses to gaze at and obey them: as at "My Cid, with the fleecy beard," in Toledo; or Bruce, as Barbour reports him; as blind old Dandolo, elected Doge at eighty-four years, storming Constantinople at ninety-four, and after the revolt again victorious and elected at the age of ninety-six to the throne of the Eastern Empire, which he declined, and died Doge at ninety-seven. We still feel the force of Socrates, "whom

well-advised the oracle pronounced wisest of men;"
of Archimedes, holding Syracuse against the Romans by his wit, and himself better than all their
nation; of Michel Angelo, wearing the four crowns
of architecture, sculpture, painting, and poetry; of
Galileo, of whose blindness Castelli said, "The noblest eye is darkened that Nature ever made, — an
eye that hath seen more than all that went before
him, and hath opened the eyes of all that shall
come after him;" of Newton, who made an important discovery for every one of his eighty-five years;
of Bacon, who "took all knowledge to be his prov-
ince;" of Fontenelle, "that precious porcelain vase
laid up in the centre of France to be guarded with
the utmost care for a hundred years;" of Franklin, Jefferson, and Adams, the wise and heroic
statesmen; of Washington, the perfect citizen; of
Wellington, the perfect soldier; of Goethe, the
all-knowing poet; of Humboldt, the encyclopædia
of science.

Under the general assertion of the well-being of
age, we can easily count particular benefits of that
condition. It has weathered the perilous capes
and shoals in the sea whereon we sail, and the
chief evil of life is taken away in removing the
grounds of fear. The insurance of a ship expires
as she enters the harbor at home. It were strange
if a man should turn his sixtieth year without a

feeling of immense relief from the number of dangers he has escaped. When the old wife says, 'Take care of that tumor in your shoulder, perhaps it is cancerous,' — he replies, 'I am yielding to a surer decomposition.' The humorous thief who drank a pot of beer at the gallows blew off the froth because he had heard it was unhealthy; but it will not add a pang to the prisoner marched out to be shot, to assure him that the pain in his knee threatens mortification. When the pleuro-pneumonia of the cows raged, the butchers said that though the acute degree was novel, there never was a time when this disease did not occur among cattle. All men carry seeds of all distempers through life latent, and we die without developing them; such is the affirmative force of the constitution; but if you are enfeebled by any cause, some of these sleeping seeds start and open. Meantime, at every stage we lose a foe. At fifty years, 'tis said, afflicted citizens lose their sick-headaches. I hope this *hegira* is not as movable a feast as that one I annually look for, when the horticulturists assure me that the rose-bugs in our gardens disappear on the tenth of July; they stay a fortnight later in mine. But be it as it may with the sick-headache, — 'tis certain that graver headaches and heart-aches are lulled once for all as we come up with certain goals of time. The passions have answered their pur-

pose : that slight but dread overweight with which
in each instance Nature secures the execution of
her aim, drops off. To keep man in the planet,
she impresses the terror of death. To perfect the
commissariat, she implants in each a certain rapac-
ity to get the supply, and a little oversupply, of
his wants. To insure the existence of the race, she
reinforces the sexual instinct, at the risk of disor-
der, grief, and pain. To secure strength, she plants
cruel hunger and thirst, which so easily overdo
their office, and invite disease. But these temporary stays and shifts for the protection of the young
animal are shed as fast as they can be replaced by
nobler resources. We live in youth amidst this
rabble of passions, quite too tender, quite too hungry and irritable. Later, the interiors of mind and
heart open, and supply grander motives. We learn
the fatal compensations that wait on every act.
Then, one after another, this riotous time-destroy-
ing crew disappear.

I count it another capital advantage of age, this,
that a success more or less signifies nothing. Little by little it has amassed such a fund of merit
that it can very well afford to go on its credit when
it will. When I chanced to meet the poet Wordsworth, then sixty-three years old, he told me that
" he had just had a fall and lost a tooth, and when
his companions were much concerned for the mis-

chance, he had replied that he was glad it had not
happened forty years before." Well, Nature takes
care that we shall not lose our organs forty years
too soon. A lawyer argued a cause yesterday in
the Supreme Court, and I was struck with a certain
air of levity and defiance which vastly became him.
Thirty years ago it was a serious concern to him
whether his pleading was good and effective. Now
it is of importance to his client, but of none to
himself. It has been long already fixed what he
can do and cannot do, and his reputation does not
gain or suffer from one or a dozen new performances. If he should on a new occasion rise quite
beyond his mark and achieve somewhat great and
extraordinary, that, of course, would instantly tell;
but he may go below his mark with impunity, and
people will say, 'O, he had headache,' or 'He lost
his sleep for two nights.' What a lust of appearance, what a load of anxieties that once degraded
him he is thus rid of! Every one is sensible of
this cumulative advantage in living. All the good
days behind him are sponsors, who speak for him
when he is silent, pay for him when he has no
money, introduce him where he has no letters, and
work for him when he sleeps.

A third felicity of age is that it has found expression. The youth suffers not only from ungrati-
fied desires, but from powers untried, and from a

picture in his mind of a career which has as yet no
outward reality. He is tormented with the want
of correspondence between things and thoughts.
Michel Angelo's head is full of masculine and
gigantic figures as gods walking, which make him
savage until his furious chisel can render them into
marble; and of architectural dreams, until a hundred stone-masons can lay them in courses of trav-
ertine. There is the like tempest in every good
head in which some great benefit for the world is
planted. The throes continue until the child is
born. Every faculty new to each man thus goads
him and drives him out into doleful deserts until it
finds proper vent. All the functions of human
duty irritate and lash him forward, bemoaning
and chiding, until they are performed. He wants
friends, employment, knowledge, power, house and
land, wife and children, honor and fame; he has
religious wants, æsthetic wants, domestic, civil, hu-
mane wants. One by one, day after day, he learns
to coin his wishes into facts. He has his calling,
homestead, social connection and personal power,
and thus, at the end of fifty years, his soul is ap-
peased by seeing some sort of correspondence between his wish and his possession. This makes
the value of age, the satisfaction it slowly offers to
every craving. He is serene who does not feel
himself pinched and wronged, but whose condition,

in particular and in general, allows the utterance
of his mind. In old persons, when thus fully expressed, we often observe a fair, plump, perennial,
waxen complexion, which indicates that all the fer-
ment of earlier days· has subsided into serenity of
thought and behavior.

The compensations of Nature play in age as in
youth. In a world so charged and sparkling with
power, a man does not live long and actively without costly additions of experience, which, though
not spoken, are recorded in his mind. What to the
youth is only a guess or a hope, is in the veteran a
digested statute. He beholds the feats of the juniors with complacency, but as one who having long
ago known these games, has refined them into results and morals. The Indian Red Jacket, when
the young braves were boasting their deeds, said,
" But the sixties have all the twenties and forties
in them."

For a fourth benefit, age sets its house in order,
and finishes its works, which to every artist is a
supreme pleasure. Youth has an excess of sensibility, before which every object glitters and attracts.
We leave one pursuit for another, and the young
man's year is a heap of beginnings. At the end
of a twelvemonth, he has nothing to show for it, —
not one completed work. But the time is not lost.
Our instincts drove us to hive innumerable experi-

ences, that are yet of no visible value, and which
we may keep for twice seven years before they
shall be wanted. The best things are of secular
growth. The instinct of classifying marks the wise
and healthy mind. Linnæus projects his system,
and lays out his twenty-four classes of plants, before yet he has found in Nature a single plant to
justify certain of his classes. His seventh class
has not one. In process of time, he finds with delight the little white *Trientalis*, the only plant with
seven petals and sometimes seven stamens, which
constitutes a seventh class in conformity with his
system. The conchologist builds his cabinet whilst
as yet he has few shells. He labels shelves for
classes, cells for species : all but a few are empty.
But every year fills some blanks, and with accelerat-
ing speed as he becomes knowing and known. An
old scholar finds keen delight in verifying the impressive anecdotes and citations he has met with in
miscellaneous reading and hearing, in all the years
of youth. We carry in memory important anecdotes, and have lost all clew to the author from
whom we had them. We have a heroic speech from
Rome or Greece, but cannot fix it on the man who
said it. We have an admirable line worthy of
Horace, ever and anon resounding in our mind's
ear, but have searched all probable and improbable
books for it in vain. We consult the reading men:

but, strangely enough, they who know everything
know not this. But especially we have a certain
insulated thought, which haunts us, but remains insulated and barren. Well, there is nothing for all
this but patience and time. Time, yes, that is the
finder, the unweariable explorer, not subject to casualties, omniscient at last. The day comes when
the hidden author of our story is found ; when the
brave speech returns straight to the hero who said
it ; when the admirable verse finds the poet to
whom it belongs ; and best of all, when the lonely
thought, which seemed so wise, yet half-wise, half-
thought, because it cast no light abroad, is suddenly
matched in our mind by its twin, by its sequence,
or next related analogy, which gives it instantly
radiating power, and justifies the superstitious instinct with which we have hoarded it. We remember our old Greek Professor at Cambridge,
an ancient bachelor, amid his folios, possessed by
this hope of completing a task, with nothing to
break his leisure after the three hours of his daily
classes, yet ever restlessly stroking his leg and as-
suring himself " he should retire from the University and read the authors." In Goethe's Romance,
Makaria, the central figure for wisdom and influence, pleases herself with withdrawing into solitude to astronomy and epistolary correspondence.
Goethe himself carried this completion of studies

to the highest point. Many of his works hung on
the easel from youth to age, and received a stroke
in every month or year. A literary astrologer, he
never applied himself to any task but at the happy
moment when all the stars consented. Bentley
thought himself likely to live till fourscore, — long
enough to read everything that was worth reading,
— "*Et tunc magna mei sub terris ibit imago.*"
Much wider is spread the pleasure which old men
take in completing their secular affairs, the inventor his inventions, the agriculturist his experiments, and all old men in finishing their houses,
rounding their estates, clearing their titles, reducing tangled interests to order, reconciling enmities,
and leaving all in the best posture for the future.
It must be believed that there is a proportion between the designs of a man and the length of his
life : there is a calendar of his years, so of his performances.

America is the country of young men, and too
full of work hitherto for leisure and tranquillity ;
yet we have had robust centenarians, and examples
of dignity and wisdom. I have lately found in an
old note-book a record of a visit to ex-President
John Adams, in 1825, soon after the election of his
son to the Presidency. It is but a sketch, and
nothing important passed in the conversation ; but
it reports a moment in the life of a heroic person,

who, in extreme old age, appeared still erect and worthy of his fame.

———, *Feb.*, 1825. To-day at Quincy, with my brother, by invitation of Mr. Adams's family. The old President sat in a large stuffed arm-chair, dressed in a blue coat, black small-clothes, white stockings ; a cotton cap covered his bald head. We made our compliment, told him he must let us join our congratulations to those of the nation on the happiness of his house. He thanked us, and said : " I am rejoiced, because the nation is happy. The time of gratulation and congratulations is nearly over with me ; I am astonished that I have lived to see and know of this event. I have lived now nearly a century ; [he was ninety in the following October ;] a long, harassed, and distracted life." I said, " The world thinks a good deal of joy has been mixed with it." — " The world does not know," he replied, " how much toil, anxiety, and sorrow I have suffered." — I asked if Mr. Adams's letter of acceptance had been read to him. — " Yes," he said, and added, " My son has more political prudence than any man that I know who has existed in my time ; he never was put off his guard ; and I hope he will continue such : but what effect age may work in diminishing the power of his mind, I do not know ; it has been very much

on the stretch, ever since he was born. He has always been laborious, child and man, from infancy."
— When Mr. J. Q. Adams's age was mentioned,
he said, " He is now fifty-eight, or will be in July;"
and remarked that " all the Presidents were of the
same age : General Washington was about fifty-
eight, and I was about fifty-eight, and Mr. Jefferson, and Mr. Madison, and Mr. Monroe." — We
inquired when he expected to see Mr. Adams. —
He said : " Never : Mr. Adams will not come to
Quincy but to my funeral. It would be a great
satisfaction to me to see him, but I don't wish him
to come on my account." He spoke of Mr. Lech-
mere, whom he " well remembered to have seen
come down daily, at a great age, to walk in the old
town-house," adding, " And I wish I could walk
as well as he did. He was Collector of the Customs for many years under the Royal Government." — E. said : " I suppose, sir, you would not
have taken his place, even to walk as well as he."—
" No, " he replied, " that was not what I wanted."
— He talked of Whitefield, and remembered when
he was a Freshman in College to have come into
town to the *Old South* church, [I think,] to hear
him, but could not get into the house ; — " I however, saw him," he said, " through a window, and
distinctly heard all. He had a voice such as I
never heard before or since. He cast it out so that

you might hear it at the meeting-house," [pointing towards the Quincy meeting-house,] "and he had the grace of a dancing-master, of an actor of plays. His voice and manner helped him more than his sermons. I went with Jonathan Sewall." — "And you were pleased with him, sir?" — "Pleased! I was delighted beyond measure." — We asked if at Whitefield's return the same popularity continued. — "Not the same fury," he said, "not the same wild enthusiasm as before, but a greater esteem, as he became more known. He did not terrify, but was admired."

We spent about an hour in his room. He speaks very distinctly for so old a man, enters bravely into long sentences, which are interrupted by want of breath, but carries them invariably to a conclusion, without correcting a word.

He spoke of the new novels of Cooper, and "Peep at the Pilgrims," and "Saratoga," with praise, and named with accuracy the characters in them. He likes to have a person always reading to him, or company talking in his room, and is better the next day after having visitors in his chamber from morning to night.

He received a premature report of his son's election, on Sunday afternoon, without any excitement, and told the reporter he had been hoaxed, for it was not yet time for any news to arrive. The

informer, something damped in his heart, insisted
on repairing to the meeting-house, and proclaimed
it aloud to the congregation, who were so over-
joyed that they rose in their seats and cheered
thrice.   The Reverend Mr. Whitney dismissed
them immediately.

When life has been well spent, age is a loss of
what it can well spare, — muscular strength, organic instincts, gross bulk, and works that belong
to these.   But the central wisdom, which was old
in infancy, is young in fourscore years, and, drop-
ping off obstructions, leaves in happy subjects the
mind purified and wise.   I have heard that whoever loves is in no condition old.   I have heard
that whenever the name of man is spoken, the doctrine of immortality is announced ; it cleaves to his
constitution.   The mode of it baffles our wit, and
no whisper comes to us from the other side.   But
the inference from the working of intellect, living
knowledge, hiving skill, — at the end of life just
ready to be born, — affirms the inspirations of affection and of the moral sentiment.

COSIMO CLASSICS

COSIMO is an innovative publisher of books and publications that inspire, inform and engage readers worldwide. Our titles are drawn from a range of subjects including health, business, philosophy, history, science and sacred texts. We specialize in using print-on-demand technology (POD), making it possible to publish books for both general and specialized audiences and to keep books in print indefinitely. With POD technology new titles can reach their audiences faster and more efficiently than with traditional publishing.

> ➤ **Permanent Availability:** Our books & publications never go out-of-print.

> ➤ **Global Availability:** Our books are always available online at popular retailers and can be ordered from your favorite local bookstore.

COSIMO CLASSICS brings to life unique, rare, out-of-print classics representing subjects as diverse as *Alternative Health, Business and Economics, Eastern Philosophy, Personal Growth, Mythology, Philosophy, Sacred Texts, Science, Spirituality* and much more!

COSIMO-on-DEMAND publishes your books, publications and reports. If you are an Author, part of an Organization, or a Benefactor with a publishing project and would like to bring books back into print, publish new books fast and effectively, would like your publications, books, training guides, and conference reports to be made available to your members and wider audiences around the world, we can assist you with your publishing needs.

Visit our website at www.cosimobooks.com to learn more about Cosimo, browse our catalog, take part in surveys or campaigns, and sign-up for our newsletter.

And if you wish please drop us a line at info@cosimobooks.com. We look forward to hearing from you.